S0-BRJ-545

RESTLESS
— in —
CHRIST

I f we are to live our lives fully and well, we must learn to embrace the opposites, to live in a creative tension between our limits and our potentials. We must honor our limitations in ways that do not distort our nature, and we must trust and use our gifts in ways that fulfill the potentials God gave us. We must take the no of the way that closes and find the guidance it has to offer — and take the yes of the way that opens and respond with the yes of our lives."

—Parker Palmer, *Let Your Life Speak*

T he next day John again was standing with two of his disciples, and as he watched Jesus walk by, he exclaimed, "Look, here is the Lamb of God!" The two disciples heard him say this, and they followed Jesus. When Jesus turned and saw them following, he said to them, "What are you looking for?" They said to him, "Rabbi (which translated means Teacher), where are you staying?" He said to them, "Come and see."   —John 1:35–39 (NRSV)

RESTLESS
— in —
CHRIST

Answering the Call to
Spiritual Commitment

SARAH STOCKTON

A Crossroad Carlisle Book
The Crossroad Publishing Company
New York

BV
5053
.S76
2004

The Crossroad Publishing Company
16 Penn Plaza, 481 Eighth Avenue
New York, NY 10001

Copyright © 2004 by Sarah Stockton

All rights reserved. No part of this book may be reproduced, stored in a retrieval system, or transmitted, in any form or by any means, electronic, mechanical, photocopying, recording, or otherwise, without the written permission of The Crossroad Publishing Company.

The text is set in 9/15.5 Leawood. Display fonts are Leawood, Optima, and Bitstream Calligraphic 421.

Printed in the United States of America

Library of Congress Cataloging-in-Publication Data
Stockton, Sarah.
  Restless in Christ : answering the call to spiritual commitment / Sarah Stockton.
    p. cm.
"A Crossroad Carlisle book."
Includes bibliographical references.
ISBN 0-8245-2253-2 (alk. paper)
  1. Spiritual direction. I. Title.
BV5053.S76 2004
253.5'3 – dc22

2004000046

1   2   3   4   5   6   7   8   9   10   10   09   08   07   06   05   04

To Andy

*who by his faithful presence
in our life together as a family,
blesses us with his love, wisdom,
good humor, and fierce and gentle spirit*

Contents

A Word from the Author

*The wind blows where it chooses, and you hear the sound of it,
but you do not know where it comes from or where it goes. So
it is with every one who is born of the Spirit.* —John 3:8

When I first met with my spiritual director, I just knew she would
say something that would make me cry, and so I braced myself
against any attempts to unnerve me. I'd read about the practice
of spiritual direction and knew the focus was on "going deep"
into the experience of God. I wanted this for myself, and yet I
didn't; I hovered between longing and rejection. Sure enough,
about half an hour into the meeting, she gently suggested that
perhaps God wanted to communicate with me just as much as I
wanted to communicate with God, and the tears welled up in spite
of my best attempts to feign indifference. Not for long though, because I changed the subject to something emotionally much safer:
complaining about the church.

That was quite a while ago. Now, during our monthly meetings, I reach for the tissue and keep talking through the tears,
though more often these days, we laugh. We explore the possibility that God might want me to feel comforted, encouraged, and
even loved. Together, we look for ways that God might be communicating this message to me. I've decided that God is the master
of subtlety. No bolts of lightning, but quiet reassurances: words

spoken through a stranger, a feeling of peace with a decision made, an inner nudging toward a life focused on the spiritual.

My spiritual director listens with open countenance and open heart as I grapple with my own resistance to God's intimate presence. Because my spirituality is relational in nature and my faith tradition is Christian, sometimes she points out a correlation between my journey and that of Christ when I ask her for help in seeing my struggles in a larger context. I want to be brought out of the isolation chamber of my own self-centered mind and into God's presence. To use a spiritual direction term: she *companions* me along the way. We have made a commitment to each other and to the Holy Spirit.

Along with being a "directee," I'm also an intern in the Spiritual Director's Institute at the Mercy Center in Burlingame, California, a three-year training program for spiritual directors. Around twenty-five of us gather in a room for monthly workshops to practice, as the program director Sister Lorita puts it, "the process of discernment." Although some of the program directors are nuns and the Mercy Center is Roman Catholic, we find as we get to know each other that we are a diverse group. Among us are Protestant pastors, rabbis, priests, nuns, Muslims, and some who practice Eastern traditions. We are married, single, partnered, celibate. Our willingness, indeed our eagerness, to explore ways of discerning the presence of the Spirit in our lives, and learning how to help others do the same, is our common bond.

In this book I offer up my own life experience of seeking God as well as my experience of spiritual direction, both as a directee and a director-in-training, and what some of the milestones and detours have been along the way toward spiritual commitment.

Christ Visits

Now when the woman saw that she was not hidden, she came trembling; and falling down before Him, she declared to Him in the presence of all the people the reason she had touched Him and how she was healed immediately. —Luke 8:47

The training supervisors in our spiritual direction program counsel that when we meet with directees we must be prepared to encounter all aspects of the human experience. We practice non-judgmental listening with others in order to notice and prevent our human impulse to back away from their emotional, spiritual, or psychological pain (and ours) from taking over, much as we practice not moving away from God. We practice not avoiding the possibility of pain and more than that, we practice staying with it, even moving more deeply into the experience, if that is what the directee, and God, wants.

I am beginning to see that my ability to be with people in the midst of their humanness both reflects and justifies my lifelong impulse to take risks in my own life. I have placed myself in the midst of all sorts of human experiences and because of that, there is little that shocks or dismays me, at least not enough to cause me to turn away from someone who needs to share his or her story. I understand. I can relate to feeling mired in sloth, envy, and greed. I have known despair, hatred, and lust. I sympathize with impatience, confusion, and resentment. I have also witnessed transformation, in myself and others; loved fervently, and been transfixed with joy. Bring on the human experience, I think to myself. I welcome it. Yet as I begin my internship, I discover that what I am unprepared for as a director-in-training while listening to my directees is Christ showing up.

Lois came to see me for a direction session at ten o'clock on a Monday morning. My living room looks nice, I thought to myself, as I bustled around getting ready for her. I shut the doors to my kids' rooms, dusted under the furniture, and closed the blinds slightly against the morning sun. When she arrived, I greeted her at the door and lit a candle on the small table between our chairs. We settled in and she began to talk, while I interjected a question or a comment here and there. Mostly though, I listened. I know how to be attentive when people are talking to me. I have been practicing this skill since I was a small child in a chaotic household. My sister, older than me by two years, was born deaf; my brother, a year and a half younger than me, was born hard of hearing. My parents were unhappily married, and the challenge of raising two hearing-impaired children strained their incompatibility even further. As the middle child, I honed my skills at translating and negotiating and tried to be heard myself, but mostly I learned how to listen: to words clumsily vocalized as my siblings struggled to speak; to emotional undercurrents; to the sound of my parents arguing in the other room. In later years I practiced these same listening skills with my ex-husband, listening for the telltale change in tone when he called to say he'd be late; listening for my children in case they woke up while he and I were arguing, and listening to him articulate his feelings as he struggled toward and achieved recovery. I can tell the difference between dissembling, evasiveness, grandiosity, and the truth. My finely tuned hearing has also brought me much pleasure. I learned how to follow complicated symphonic orchestration in music classes, and I can hear the quivering in my children's voices when they are excited or awed. I can recognize authentic emotion in another's voice.

I discover that what I am unprepared for
as a director-in-training while listening to
my directees is Christ showing up.

This particular day, as I follow Lois's words, I am visualizing the scenes she describes and empathizing with her story. I go wholeheartedly into her experience. As she describes her ritual of reading the Sunday morning paper, I imagine her seated on the living room floor, surrounded by sections of the paper. Her family comes into the room, wanting her attention. She tries to focus on the paper, her husband, and her daughter all at the same time. She feels overwhelmed by the needs of everyone in the room, including herself. I see her sitting there, the paper spread out, feeling frustrated. When she pauses for a moment, I suddenly see, or sense, something else. I see Christ. I don't mean I literally see him, a person standing there, or rather, next to her on the floor, reading the paper with her, but I have a very strong sense that Christ is there with her. But I am the one who senses this. So what does that mean for me? What is Christ offering me? Instead of letting myself be distracted by this new experience, I return to Lois and her story. Later, in supervision, I will learn that this was the moment I could have, should have stayed with, following Christ's lead into the heart of her experience. Right then in that moment all I did was notice, which was a start.

13

A week or so later I described this sensation in a small group during a spiritual direction workshop. "So it seemed like maybe, somehow, it could have been that Christ was there," I said hesitantly, equivocating in the group setting, when I knew perfectly well that the experience had left no room for doubt or equivocation in my heart. "What was that?" I asked, as I turned to the workshop supervisor, a woman I trust implicitly to tell me the truth.

"That was Christ," she responded matter-of-factly, and were she in her teens instead of her sixties, she might have added, "duh."

In all of my history of listening, there have been a few times when it felt as though God had showed up, though I didn't recognize it as such then. During Al-Anon meetings, for instance, it often felt like something greater than ourselves was present, heightening the intimacy of the sharing. Sometimes it happens when I hear the Sunday liturgy, or when someone is telling me something particularly important, close to the heart, risking their trust in me. A sensation comes over me as if the very blood in my veins carries new energy; the space we are abiding in begins to warm; each part of my body feels embraced. This experience with the Sunday paper and Christ was a new one, though. I both felt it and visualized it as though a veil had been lifted.

What did I say to Lois? Nothing — it wasn't her experience, it was mine, and I didn't want to superimpose my insight onto her human experience. I also didn't know what to do with that experience, so I let it pass. I did ask her, though, if she might be willing to consider, next time she was reading the Sunday paper and wondering how to feel less crowded, if she might try asking Christ to help her with her feelings, to guide her in what to do. She seemed willing to try this, intrigued at the thought. I carried that image of Christ on the floor of the living room around with me for days, wondering what might come next, hoping for more.

A Reluctant Detour

But he said, O my Lord, please send someone else.
—Exodus 4:13

The first year of my training in spiritual direction I often felt so rest-less, so stirred up by my grief-filled response to God's call that at times I found it difficult to remain composed. This was especially true any time we weren't discussing topics in a more abstract way, when I could distract myself by taking notes and asking questions. But I couldn't distract myself during prayer rituals when we were asked to embrace the beckoning tug of our feelings and express whatever was stirring in us at that moment. While most of the par-ticipants would share feelings of peace or hope or gratitude, I more often would cry my way through the lighting of the candles or as we passed an icon around hand to hand, shaken by an overwhelm-ing sense of the years I had spent feeling bereft and abandoned, restless yet undirected, stumbling toward hope. I grieved for the shut-down child I had been and for the subsequent years spent struggling to identify who I might become and how I might live. Alternating between a kind of emotional sleepwalking and taking wanton risks, I was unable to recognize or respond to God's gentle hand on my shoulder, sometimes avoiding God's gaze defiantly, other times out of ignorance and obliviousness. During that first year of training I allowed my restlessness and grief full expression by acknowledging it, feeling it, and talking about it. It helped me to stay fully present to each movement of my heart. Acknowledging my restless spirit meant confronting myself and God. As I did, my heart opened up.

At the end of the year, someone from the direction training committee called to tell me they had decided I wasn't ready to go on to the second year. They felt I wasn't ready to begin directing others as part of the practicum portion of the second-year training. I was stunned. I didn't know how to defend myself, how to advocate for myself, although I believed they were wrong to let me go. I strongly believed, and still do, that the way I experienced the first year was authentic and valid, that I was actually living out what they were talking about in all of the training sessions. The goal of a good spiritual director, after all, is to facilitate a direct relationship between the directee and God. I had been practicing my own direct relationship for the entire year. I felt like there was some unspoken hierarchy of spiritual achievement that I should have accomplished, the equivalent of making it to some spiritual mountaintop. I guess they perceived me as still grappling my way up the mountainside, not ready to companion anyone else on the journey.

I was knocked off my feet by that phone call, and I cried on and off for days. I spent the next several months questioning my own experience, my own intuitive feelings about the wisdom of my participation in the training. And I got mad at myself. Why did I always need to cause trouble by speaking up? Why couldn't I leave well enough alone, participate silently, even pretend a serenity I didn't feel, or at least not admit its absence? I felt humiliated, angry, misunderstood, and upset. If we are supposed to see the movement of God in all situations, what did this situation tell me? That God rejected me as a spiritual director? These thoughts lessened as time went on and I talked with my husband and with spiritual directors from other programs, and consulted my own heart. I explored other paths, trained in creativity coaching, started my own website on creativity and the spirit, became more involved in my church. I wrote and prayed and raged at God, and I began to make peace with what had happened.

> Acknowledging my restless spirit meant confronting myself and God. As I did, my heart opened up.

I knew I had progressed down the path of spiritual direction too far to want to turn away. I could pretend I didn't care, that I didn't want to practice helping others be in close relationship with God, that I was content to do other things. But it wasn't true. I longed for more meaningful work. I missed it very much. Besides, I kept running into the director of the program at odd moments, which was very disconcerting. What did it mean? I told her, finally, how I felt, how I still grieved for the lost opportunity to learn how to be a spiritual director. It felt wrong, I told her, not to pursue this calling, as my tears welled up. "The door isn't closed," she said to me one day, as we stood outside the church where we had both just attended a service. "Why don't you come talk to me sometime? Things change." Did she mean me, or them? Or both?

I decided to try and look at the year away as a detour, not a dead end. And so I went back. I had to interview again and talk about why I felt I was ready to go on into the second year. I had to justify my longing, and myself. I had to ask to come back into the program, and it was very difficult. I had to own my part in it, to examine where I might have some spiritual growing up to do. What I didn't say was that I had gotten around my own hurt pride by reframing the experience of discerning whether or not I am called to be a spiritual director as something between me and God, not between me and the program leaders. The training is just a means to an end, I told myself, and I will keep my own spiritual angst in check this time around, saving that for my conversations with God. I also didn't say out loud that over that year of being on my own, part of me had been relieved to be away from the intensity of the program. The invitation to go into the unknown, to connect with God, had often been painful, as they well knew, and that had not entirely changed. Christ and I had reached a grudging standoff more often than not. Still, all things considered, I wanted to go on.

That first day back at the program, starting my second year with a new group, seeing people at lunchtime from my old group, people who had now progressed beyond me in the training, was painful. I spent most of the day so tightly wound I could feel my heart pounding and I also had a massive headache. I didn't start crying until I drove home, exhausted by the day, by my life. Keeping the heart open, my eyes open for a glimpse of Christ, accepting instead of rejecting the belated invitation, was hard. I chose a path committed to conscious participation in a relationship with the Holy Spirit. For most of my life, it has felt like God has chosen me, calling on me to volunteer even though I didn't have my hand up. At first a reluctant recruit, I now find myself driven by a hunger for more.

God

A Retrospective

The word of the Lord was rare in those days; visions were not widespread. — 1 Samuel 3:1

One afternoon during a spiritual direction workshop on an autumn Saturday, as the slanting sun warmed the large room where we were gathered, we were asked to chart what the leader referred to as our "graced history." As I understood it, they wanted us to come up with a brief spiritual autobiography. They didn't directly specify that we start with our earliest memories, which was fortunate, because I'm flummoxed when I try to come up with examples of God's presence from my childhood or adolescence. I feel like I'm lucky to have experienced such graced moments in the last few years (and sometimes I'm uncertain if I've even done that), never mind in my more distant past. Instead of delighting in remembering those supposedly graced moments, I was visited by the girl I once was: floundering, making things up as I went along, taking heedless risks. In fact, most of my memories from any part of my life except for the last few years could be listed under the heading, "What was I thinking?"

There was the time I improvised a dance to "Born to Be Wild" in the fourth-grade talent show in 1969. Was that a graced moment? I half-admire and half-cringe when I think of that little girl now, so fearlessly and foolishly dancing and leaping about on stage, with no practice, no script, no plan. This past year, my eleven-year-old daughter sang "I Love Rock and Roll" on stage in front of an enthusiastic audience at her school talent show. She was poised, practiced, funny, and polished. My daughter thrives on attention, radiates well-being, and is infused with creative spirit, and with God. She is surrounded by love. We, that is, my daughter now and my girl-self then, share the same impulse to perform, to express our enthusiasm, our delight at being able to sing and dance. Yet when I compared these two girls side by side in my mind, my younger self and my present-day daughter, I remembered the child I was as lonely and alone. I didn't write this memory down on my chart.

I realize now as I listen to people sharing
their own graced histories that God shows
up in my life in the struggles and the risks.

I reached for another memory, "perhaps something in nature," the leader suggested. I remember my high school years, living in Southern California. When my mother and brother and I first moved to Laguna Beach, I was afraid of the ocean. The ocean might look benevolent from the shore, but I knew the terror of being lifted up and slammed down to the ocean floor, tumbled over and over in the green haze, only to dredge myself up on to the beach with scraped knees, sinuses full of salt water. I quickly realized, however, that the sea, which was never more than a few blocks away from where I lived, went to school, or hung out with friends, couldn't be avoided. It formed the backdrop of all teenage social life. I had to conquer my fear if I wanted to fit in, and I desperately wanted to fit in. It seemed like the waves relentlessly taunted me, reminding me of my fear, never completely silent, never consistent. Yet I was taunting myself as I projected my inner struggle onto the great, abiding sea. However I might align myself with the ocean, it never aligned itself with me, disregarding my presence as so much flotsam. In fact, disregarding or regarding didn't enter into it. The sea is a neutral force, moving with energy but without any aspect of thought or deliberate intention.

That fall afternoon, sitting in a peaceful room in Northern California, in my mind I watched my teenage self developing a strategy for conquering her antagonist. Up every morning before school, I made my way down to the beach. I observed that the waves are calmest in the early morning, the water often smooth and glassy. I learned that the presence of surfers bobbing on the water meant those were the places where the waves are the most numerous, so I headed down the beach away from their territory, to where the water lapped and hissed on the sand. I crouched on the edge of the waves for several minutes, watching for the morning's rhythm. Do the sets roll in three at a time, or four? Does the water pull back underneath the next set in a sucking motion, or does it whirl sideways back from the shore? When I had tuned my own staccato heart rhythm to the alternating beat of the waves, I leapt up and ran into the water, diving under the first wave then up to the surface again quickly, striking out for the further distance, out past the swells.

I performed this ritual time and again, most days of the year, for three years. Once in, the sea, while never my friend, became a wordless source of comfort. I left insecurity, anxiety, shame, desire, on the shore. In the water I was complete. I never actually feared *water;* it was the waves that frightened me, in their power to toss me about with neutral and fierce abandon. Yet once in the water, I knew I had conquered my fear of the waves once again by diving headlong into what I feared and swimming out past it.

Back in the present moment, in my forty-three-year-old self, I decided to chart this as a graced moment, though it was more like a graced relationship emerging over time with myself, with the sea, with my inner compulsion to conquer what I fear, and to embrace what lies beyond what I fear. I realize now as I listen to people sharing their own graced histories that God shows up in my life in the struggles and the risks. Maybe God is there in a little girl's desire to dance as she braves the stage. And maybe God is there again, diving with me through the waves. As the afternoon waned and the workshop wound down, I felt grateful for this new interpretation of my past. Yet I also continue to feel a compassionate sadness for the dancer and the swimmer who may have been with God, but didn't know it at the time.

Spiritual Direction, an Overview

Historically, spiritual direction in the Christian faith tradition was mainly available for those in religious life or thinking about entering religious life, usually in a seminary or convent setting. Spiritual directors were those already in religious vocations who felt called to direct others on the spiritual journey. Those seeking spiritual direction would meet regularly with a priest or pastor to help determine whether they had a "calling" to the vocation of religious life. Once committed to such a path, they might continue in spiritual direction as a means of ongoing spiritual discernment. Nowadays, for laypeople (those members of a religious tradition who are not part of the clergy or in religious orders, but are members of a congregation), or spiritual seekers (those who are on a spiritual path though not affiliated with a particular tradition), it might summon up an image of pastoral counseling and support for those times when you reach important milestones like marriage, or need help facing a terminal illness. Spiritual direction can address these questions and experiences, but it can also be much more. Over the last thirty years or so, spiritual direction has blossomed as a discipline by which those who encounter God in the fabric of their daily lives act as an attentive presence for others seeking a similar encounter. The movement has been away from "directing" someone toward "companioning" someone on the journey. As they say at the Mercy Center, "We stand poised and attentive to the movement of God in our hearts." At this present time more and more laypeople are entering spiritual direction training programs as they begin to recognize and want to explore their own calling to this spiritual vocation.

So what does spiritual direction look like? Typically, you meet once a month, sometimes more often, depending on need. As in psychotherapy, you meet for an hour. All human experience is appropriate and rich content for spiritual direction, because we seek God in all human experience. Unlike most traditional therapy sessions, however, the emphasis is not on solutions to problems, but rather on discerning your relationship with God within those human experiences. The focus remains on the spiritual, and a good director acts as a kind of trail guide as together you travel the path of your life, noticing and pointing out the signs of God's presence along the way: a broken tree branch here, a bird persistently calling over there. A spiritual director won't make life decisions for you, or replace your theology with hers. Instead, she offers unconditional love, nonjudgmental and attentive listening, commitment to the process, a prayerful vehicle for God's presence, and gentle guidance toward spiritual clarity.

———————

Over the last thirty years or so, spiritual direction has blossomed as a discipline by which those who encounter God in the fabric of their daily lives act as an attentive presence for others seeking a similar encounter. The movement has been away from "directing" someone toward "companioning" someone on the journey.

———————

Spiritual directors are no longer to be found only among the ranks of the clergy or other professional religious. There are many centers for training worldwide, and you will find some resources at the back of this book. An extensive body of literature also exists for reading about everything from the history of spiritual direction to ethical issues, interfaith practice, pagan mentoring, feminist spiritual direction, and more. Although an examination of the membership statistics for Spiritual Directors International shows a preponderance of directors from the Roman Catholic tradition, with Protestants running a close second, there has recently been more emphasis in training programs and in literature on interfaith awareness and other religious practices, including Buddhist, Jewish, Muslim, and Native American spirituality.

Ideally, spiritual direction provides a safe place to speak openly about God with someone who is closely listening. The director's job is to invite God into the room, to embody God's love, compassion, and attentiveness, and to act as a companion as you begin to look for God along the path of your life.

A Teenage Creed

The Lord looks down from heaven on humankind to see if there are any who are wise, who seek after God.   —Psalm 14:2

Once a week for the past few months, I've spent the evening with a group of teenagers who are participating in confirmation preparation. I knew some of these kids by sight and by reputation before the confirmation program began, because they are a grade ahead of my son in school. The difference is that he is now at the top of the heap as an eighth-grader in middle school, and they are at the bottom as first-year students in high school. Other kids in the class are from the parish but did not attend the parish school. They tend to group together based on what high school they are now attending, which often leaves the kids from non-Christian private schools, or those who ended up at the local public school, on the social edge. I have a mixed bunch in the group of kids I'm in charge of, and it's been a challenge to get them to talk to each other beyond the level of bantering and "whatever, dude."

The writing exercise for last week's meeting asked them to "rewrite" the Nicene Creed in their own words, a traditional prayer that they have no doubt been reciting since kindergarten, probably without really thinking about what they were saying. My own small group of six kids was given the first stanza to rework. At first, it seemed like the evening would drift away while they compared cell phone covers and doodled all over the worksheets that had been handed out. As a parent of two children in a rigorously academic Christian elementary and middle school, I know these kids have worked hard at their studies for most of their young lives. Although they are privileged by most of the world's standards, they have paid a price in terms of stress and a lack of creative freedom. They seemed tired, restless, not resentful exactly (at least not overtly), but definitely resistant. I decided to stir things up.

I saw that creativity is a powerful spiritual force in the lives of teenagers.

I read the opening line of the prayer out loud, waited until I had their attention (which involved raising my voice slightly and taking away a rubber band catapult from one young man) and then said, "There must be a better way to say that."

After some blank stares and glancing sideways at each other, one quiet girl with braces and a perpetually worried brow spoke up. "Of course there is," she said softly, as I leaned a bit closer to hear her. I nodded encouragingly, not wanting to scare her off, at the same time moving my pen out of reach of the kid who kept trying to borrow it. I waited, hoping she'd go on. She looked at me to make sure I was listening, as if expecting me to give up on her. I didn't. She then offered a version of the first line that not only contained the essence of its meaning but also expanded it. I drew in my breath softly. *Yes,* I thought to myself. The other kids just looked at her. I looked around at the group and plowed on. "That's a great start. Thank you. Now, what about this next line?" I pitched my voice against the rising hum in the room, as twenty-five kids divided into small groups tried to get around what they perhaps perceived as just another school assignment. "I mean, nobody talks this way, do they? Do you guys talk this way?"

And suddenly, it happened. They focused. They became intrigued. They offered outrageous interpretations of each line, and I didn't blink. They challenged each other, made fun of each other, and in the end came up with a new version of a centuries-old prayer that stunned me. It contained their voices but retained the wisdom of their faith tradition. I praised these pimply, restless, awkward kids, told them they were creative, and then ignored them for awhile, so they could get back to their flirting and doodling.

As a fledging spiritual director, I began to wonder how teenagers might benefit from undivided attention to their spiritual process.

What did I take away from that experience? I saw how profoundly and clearly they could think, given the chance. I saw how much they remained connected to their faith tradition, even when they challenged it, reworked it, made it their own. I saw that creativity is a powerful spiritual force in the lives of teenagers. I saw myself, thirty years ago. I wondered how the course of my life would have been altered if someone had spoken seriously to me about God when I was a teenager. I thought about how I too might rework the texts that have become routine and mundane to me, in order to revitalize and reconnect my relationship with Christ. I thought about how I could rework the very text of my life. I saw that I had received the gift of hope for these kids' future, the gift of experiencing the creativity of the Holy Spirit at work. As a fledging spiritual director, I began to wonder how teenagers might benefit from undivided attention to their spiritual process.

The revised creed they came up with had some doctrinal changes that no doubt could keep seminarians and theologians busy for years dissecting the implications of each word. Yet I wasn't there to assertively challenge the theology held by these kids. There simply isn't enough time for that in an hour-and-a-half meeting once a week, with a room full of squirrelly teenagers, and besides, that wasn't my role. My hope is that they might begin to see that there are alternatives between passively not questioning that which they don't understand or dislike about their faith tradition, or bolting out of the church both in body and in spirit as soon as they have met the parental and social demand to go through the confirmation process. I figured all I could hope for was to encourage them to begin to see how the Christian faith might be made their own; that as teenagers on the edge of adulthood it might be time to identify, examine, and claim their own place in relationship with Christ.

My Father's Faith

It is no longer enough to have been born into a Christian family,
to have been baptized. . . . To have a living faith today one must
at some point in his or her life make a deep, private act of faith.

— Ronald Rolheiser, *The Holy Longing:*
The Search for a Christian Spirituality

My dad and I sat in the shade by the local community pool, watching my kids as they swam and shouted under the hot July sun. I'm in my forties now, grown up enough to start having a real relationship with my dad, or so I hope. He left California for Massachusetts when I was sixteen, and for almost thirty years, until he retired and moved back to the West a year ago, our contact had consisted of a couple of days a year when he flew out for a visit, the occasional letter or brief phone call. He had loomed large in my psyche during those years, as fathers do, absent or present. Now he seems both more tangible and less mysterious. We've had more real conversations this last year than in the last twenty-five years. A nice man, I thought to myself, as we settled into the lazy afternoon.

We watched the kids swim as we chatted about this and that and drank our Diet Cokes. After a momentary lull, he turned his chair more toward me.

"Have I ever told you about my conversion experience?" he asked. Although he had alluded to wanting to "get together and really talk," and he knew I was beginning to write about my own spiritual journey, I hadn't expected this. My dad had always been reticent about anything personal, and our conversations over the years had centered on topics like gardening. What he did for a living, the fact that he was a minister, seemed to have no bearing on our lives.

I quickly scanned my memories of the last twenty years or so. After all, I thought, if he had told me, I could scarcely admit to having forgotten something so significant, could I? But then, he doesn't remember the occasion either, so either way I'm off the hook.

"I'd like to hear it," I responded. He settled into his deck chair and gazed out over the pool to the shimmering cottonwood trees beyond. Then he launched right in to the story, as if he'd been preparing for weeks. Maybe he had. One night, he said, in his freshman year at Harvard, he had gone to a prayer meeting run by some fellows from Princeton Seminary. He had enjoyed it, but had never felt anything like the presence of Jesus that they spoke about with such earnestness. My father's Protestant background had not prepared him to hear that Christ was a living Christ, and that you could ask Jesus to come into your heart. His religious beliefs up until that point had to do with charitable works, right action, and acting for the greater good. "And all that stuff, you know," he said, looking for confirmation, as I nodded. He had gone back to his dorm room that night and had slept, only to waken in the morning with an overwhelming sense of God's love.

"A warmth, a certainty, as though the world and everything in it were heightened, filled with a graceful presence of love," he said. I tried to take in what he was saying, unable to imagine it, not skeptical exactly, but not identifying with it either.

"How long did that last?" I wanted to know.

"About twenty-four hours, I guess. It faded, and then it was gone. There was definitely a qualitative difference in how I felt during that time. I walked around feeling like everything was transformed, heightened, more beautiful, I don't know."

We sat in silence for a few moments. My daughter came up to me, dripping wet and chattering away. I let her pull me over to the side of the pool to watch her hold her breath underwater while I counted. I congratulated her, shooed her off, and went back to my chair.

My father's Protestant background had not prepared him to hear that Christ was a living Christ, and that you could ask Jesus to come into your heart.

My father looked eager to get on with his story. He talked about how he believes that such experiences of grace are not to be summoned up at will, or even because of how one conducts one's religious life, but are to be cherished as blessed yet random and haphazard events. That struck me as a very frustrating way to proceed in one's faith, hoping as I do that somehow I might eventually find a way to summon God's presence, rather than what resembled waiting by the phone for that boy that you like so much to call, when he doesn't know you exist. Mostly though, I wondered if I could take his word for it. Should I believe in this graced randomness because it's what he believes?

"And have you doubted that experience since?"

"Well, I have wondered only rarely if that really was God's presence, but no, not really disbelieved, I guess."

We gazed out toward the pool and the children splashing amid cries of "Marco" and the response "Polo." Other adults, mostly mothers, were baking themselves in the summer sun. As he told me about that time at Harvard, waking in his dorm room early in the morning, awash in the surety of God's presence and God's love, I concentrated on trying to remember the details of what he said, while simultaneously envying the feeling he was conveying to me, over forty years later. To have known, to have felt, even once, that immediate certainty! I wanted to understand, wanting to know *how it worked.*

After a brief lull we talked about theology, the Protestant church, spirituality, the latest studies on the historical life of Jesus, and books we had read on the subject, but it was an intellectual discussion, focused on how we framed our faith practice, not the unnamed and unnamable feelings at the core.

More questions came to me later, but by then we were back at his house barbecuing. The kids ran around the yard with squirt guns, and we chatted away with my husband and my dad's wife. But I wanted to know: Did he ever try to recapture that feeling? Did he pray for it fervently, feel its loss, grow discouraged?

My parents divorced when I was twelve, and my father remarried shortly thereafter and then moved from California to Massachusetts. I hardly qualify as a typical preacher's kid, since I have only a handful of memories from childhood of being in church despite years of weekly Sunday attendance, and I have only heard my dad preach a couple of times in the last twenty years or so. Yet I remember the hymns: "There Is a Balm in Gilead," "Morning Has Broken," "Faith of Our Fathers," "Jesus Christ Is Risen Today."

What had my father said all those times in church? I don't remember a word. What had he ever said about faith, about our Protestant heritage, about what he believed? What had we talked about around the Sunday dinner table, how did he feel about my spiritual upbringing, and what did it mean to be the daughter of a minister?

Not a word comes back to me. I suppose the combination of my naturally reticent father, my own habit of adapting myself to the way other people relate, and the dry and reserved nature of our religious tradition we operated within combined to form a religious legacy that left me standing at a seemingly empty well, unable to even identify my thirst, let alone seek ways to assuage it.

Until that day by the pool, any conversations we had about faith had mostly taken place through letters and then e-mail. I've never asked him the hard questions, like why he had never shared his personal beliefs with me, and how did it come to pass that I felt so abandoned in my youth and beyond, so bereft, longing for something I couldn't name, something I had no language for.

My father has lived his life as a good and faithful New England–style Protestant, practicing the Christian values of neighborliness, kindness, ethical work practices, and social awareness of human suffering and injustice. God comes to him through the byways of life: through music and sunsets, through the faces of people in his congregation, through the love of his family. If I were my dad's spiritual director, I would encourage him to explore his feelings in those experiences and whether he might more readily recognize God there. But I'm not his director. I'm his daughter, and we are busy learning about what that relationship means. I crave that visitation, that all-encompassing embrace of Christ, which my dad felt as a young man, however briefly. I wonder if having felt it once, I would be content with that.

In the Quiet

From his fullness we have all received, grace upon grace.

—John 1:16

As a spiritual director in training, I regularly meet with directees. I seem to draw people who are grappling with their own spiritual restlessness, although they may not recognize it as such, or welcome it. Recently I met with Frances, an energetic and thoughtful career woman in her early thirties, for our first direction session. She needed no prompting to begin, launching right into the spiritual dilemma occupying her. When I meet with my own director I don't hesitate either, grateful to have someone willing to listen to my ongoing internal whirl of thoughts. I even have to make myself slow down for the moment of silence my director begins each session with; I often feel like I'm waiting for her to get centered while I'm poised at the edge, waiting to dive in. Fortunately when I'm in the role of director I feel much more relaxed, ready to follow the pace set by the person sitting across from me. The restless spiritual energy that often stirs me to action also helps me focus on the present moment as a director. At such times my restless energy is being put to its rightful use, in service of the Holy Spirit.

Frances began by telling me some of her history as a member of a parish, her family history in the church, and the fact that she lives with her fiancé. She mentioned that she'd been listening to Christian radio a lot on the way to the office. She'd also been

35

reading a lot about spirituality and thought about taking a Bible studies class. Then she went on to tell me something about her friendship with a woman at work, and her struggle to live up to the Christian standard that she felt this friend had set. After we sat in silence for a few moments, contemplating this perfect friend, Frances talked some more about her childhood in the church, and then she mentioned the radio again.

"Tell me more about listening to the radio," I said, noticing how this seemingly unimportant detail kept coming up in her increasingly emotional recital. She said she'd been listening to this station in the car for the last several months, trying, as she put it, to follow the good Christian path by paying attention to the Word as interpreted by the commentators. Suddenly, one morning, feeling rebellious, she shut the radio off. She checked my reaction to what might appear from the outside as a small enough act of defiance. I nodded encouragingly, waiting for her to flesh out her experience. It obviously signified something much more profound.

"So you turned off the radio. What was that like?"

"Quiet. Uncomfortable. Quiet."

She smiled shyly and I smiled back, both of us present in the quiet.

Frances went on to share that she'd spent the whole previous week feeling out of alignment with her religious practice. It worried her, reminding her of an earlier time when her dissatisfaction with the church had driven her right out the door. She'd stayed away for years. All week, she confided, she'd been wrestling with feeling constrained by what she believed God, as voiced by the church (epitomized by the radio commentators and her more perfect friend), wanted of her, instead of what she might want for herself. She felt like she'd failed as a Christian by refusing to listen to that Christian radio station. She'd chosen the quiet of her own heart, her own thoughts. I could see that she felt shaken, but what seemed more significant to me was her willingness to stay with it, painful as it was.

Together we explored the options. She ventured one suggestion: She could try and quell her restlessness by reapplying herself to her reading and to her friend's suggestions, petitioning God for forgiveness, and asking for a peaceful spirit.

"You could do that," I said, careful not to inflect my voice, not wanting to steer her into any direction other than what felt authentically right for her.

She nodded rather glumly at this option. A second option I thought of but didn't voice: she could abandon her quest for answers and engagement and thus deny her restlessness altogether. It seemed to me that if she really wanted to avoid her restlessness and what it might ask of her, she certainly wouldn't have bothered seeking spiritual direction. Another option that we explored felt the most right to her. She decided that she would try bringing her restlessness straight to God (bypassing the more perfect friend), to ask what it meant for her. Nothing more than that, but for her, a way toward God, instead of a stepping back. An action generated by her restlessness, as seemingly small as turning off the radio, but one that makes room for infinite possibility. She relaxed into her chair and breathed into her whole body, letting go of the anxiety she had carried with her for days, perhaps even years. It felt peaceful with awareness rather than placid with denial. An infusion of spirit, rather than a diffusing of longing. Full of grace.

Fallible Teachers

Imagine what it would be like for you to believe for a day, or even an hour, that you are God's temple and that God's Spirit dwells within you, and that this makes you holy.

—Debra K. Farrington, *One Like Jesus:*
Conversations on the Single Life

Sometimes as a spiritual director I am called to teach. A theological misunderstanding may be preventing someone from seeing a way toward God. A misconception about the requirements of a faith practice or a need for new words or fresh concepts may prompt me to offer some insights or simple information that contributes to someone's current knowledge base or helps them begin their own search for more knowledge. I enjoy this aspect of my role as director, but I am not primarily a teacher. I am there to enter the mystery. Yet teachers have had a profound impact on my life and my spirituality for better or worse, and teaching is definitely an aspect of spiritual direction. I still think about the teaching path, wondering if it might have been for me if the right teacher had come along and if the wrong one hadn't.

I've always loved singing. As the perennial new student in a new school (we moved a lot), I always found a home in the school choir. In high school I sang in the general chorus, and in my sopho-more year I auditioned and was accepted into a smaller "madrigal" group. We sang early Christian hymns ("Look Down, O Lord"),

Renaissance madrigals ("Who Is at My Window, Who?"), Gregorian chants, and an occasional medieval jazzy number like "Sumer is a cumin in, Lude sing cucu." I sang second soprano, my voice not quite ethereal enough for first soprano and not quite rich enough for alto. We rehearsed several times a week and sometimes on weekends. We traveled around Southern California, performing and participating in choir festivals. We all loved our conductor, a short, rotund man I'll call Harold. He was given to flights of rapture when he discussed European architecture or long-dead composers. He taught us how to listen to classical compositions, how to focus, and how to adjust our voices to each other and to the acoustics of the room, so that we united in one pure tone of sound. We were very good, and he was a very good teacher. He made me want to teach as well, because it looked like so much fun and felt so important, so meaningful. My teenage years were all about longing, searching for meaning and for romance. The music we made came the closest to filling that need that I could find; more satisfying than a boyfriend, less fickle than social status or popularity, more reliable than family.

The summer after high-school graduation, our small choir traveled to Europe with Harold and a couple of chaperones on a singing tour. We'd held fundraisers and cajoled our parents and grandparents into paying our way. The plan was to perform in several of the great cathedrals of Europe and sing music that had been written specifically for each site, in order to fully experience the acoustical magic of the echoing stone chambers of history. As we visited each majestic site, from Lincoln Cathedral in England to Mont St. Michel and Chartres in France, I felt more and more stirred up inside. Often moved to tears without knowing why as we entered each new vaulted house of worship, I figured it must be love, or heartache, or fear for my unknown future. I never thought that it might be God. If the thought did cross my mind it quickly dissipated in the hormonal brew of being an adolescent, thinned out by a large dose of cultural cynicism. It was 1978, and in my social group our gods were music, poetry, the arts, sex, alcohol, and drugs. Looking back, I think I cried from pure longing, a girl casting about for direction. What is the way to God when you are eighteen and unsupported by a spiritual community or worse yet, embedded in a community of equally undirected, aimless souls?

I had turned eighteen during my senior year. I wrote poetry, took dance classes, thought about teaching music or writing, and sang in the local Episcopal church where our school choir director led the choir. The music we sang each Sunday was almost too beautiful to bear but impossible to stay away from. I floundered badly that year. My best friend had moved on to other friends, including a boyfriend who didn't like me around. Two of my other closest friends had graduated the year before. I wanted to be a writer, maybe an English teacher or a music teacher, but had no idea how to go about becoming one. I lived alone with my mom. We had very little money, and although it was assumed I would go to college, I had no plan for how to get there. I drank too much at parties, experimented with drugs, and cried a lot.

One consistent source of comfort was Harold and his love of music. I felt affirmed when he chose me to sing solos, and I spent a lot of after-school time hanging around his school office, talking about stuff I can't even remember now. He was smart, funny, and friendly. He seemed to think I was smart and talented, something I desperately needed to believe. I knew I didn't have the best voice. I had been trained well enough in listening by then to recognize the difference between a good voice and a professional voice. As I came to realize that I didn't have a future as a professional singer, my sense of self grew attenuated and my connection to hope grew thin. I couldn't imagine teaching; it would require self-confidence, and I had very little, just enough to get out the door in the morning, and sometimes not even that.

It was 1978, and in my social group our gods
were music, poetry, the arts, sex, alcohol,
and drugs. Looking back, I think I cried
from pure longing, a girl casting about
for direction. What is the way to God
when you are eighteen and unsupported
by a spiritual community or worse yet,
embedded in a community of equally
undirected, aimless souls?

On my eighteenth birthday, Harold took me out to a very fancy lunch which I remember to this day. We had fresh trout, warm spinach and bacon salad, and a bottle of Pouilly Fuisse wine. Oh, and a gin and tonic (or two) to start. I was literally wined and dined. On the way home, as he pulled his car up outside the apartment where my mom and I lived, he began talking about how what I needed was time away from the pressure of high school and the unhappiness and confusion I was feeling about my situation and my future. He suggested that I might benefit from some time away, from the pressures of home, school, and boyfriends (or lack thereof). I nodded along, slightly fuzzy from the wine, thinking in my naïve, eighteen-year-old way that what he was saying sounded so true, so wise. And then I finally tuned in from my alcohol-haze to his confident, "I know what's best for you" come-on.

"With you?" I asked, not believing what I was hearing.

41

He was smiling at me. I was stunned. I may have been naïve in the ways of the heart, but by eighteen I knew a come-on when I heard one. Somehow I got out of the car and into the house, and somehow I made it through the next few months and through that tour of Europe, and somehow I made it to my present, wiser age of forty-three. Twenty-five years later, I look back from my vantage point and I mourn that girl. That year I lost my belief in the power of music to transform my life and fill my deepest longing and was left with nothing to replace it. I also learned to mistrust all teachers and their intentions. I doubted my own ability to teach. I've had to unlearn my fear of following my heart, of moving toward my desire for closeness and companionship. Fortunately, I have also learned to not mistake a fallible, human music teacher for the gift of music, just as I have learned not to mistake the teacher for the *teachings*. I spent a long time after that doubting that I'd ever had any talent. Had I been chosen for solos because he wanted to seduce me? Had his choir-directing been a form of seduction only? Did he really believe in us as a choir, or was that an act?

After high school my restless need for meaning and connection kept nudging me toward some way to encounter the transcendent as I moved on, left home, and grew up.

Like an abusive priest who distorts and corrupts the message of God's love through his own salacious actions, Harold's advances tainted my experience of singing, the nearest thing to transcendence I'd had in my life until then. My poetic self grew cynical, and I lost my innocence, the stuff of wonder and dreams. Now, in my forties, I have found other paths to transcendence and other ways to experience the glory of singing. Prayer, reflection, sharing with a spiritual director and writing about it, have all led to a new contentment as I sing along with my kids as we listen to music in the car or while I cook dinner, and I cherish the many nights spent singing them to sleep as infants and small children. Singing is God's gift to me and those I love, and through the healing of God's love it's more than enough; it's grace. And teaching has reclaimed its place in my heart as a connecting thread between learner and teacher, between me and Christ.

After high school my restless need for meaning and connection kept nudging me toward some way to encounter the transcendent as I moved on, left home, and grew up. I kept looking for teachers in college and graduate school who I might trust and learn from. I found them on rare occasions, and I am grateful to them for their patience, their ability to challenge me to greater things, their compassion. Now, as a spiritual director I am finding my way again into what it means to be a teacher, as I listen to my workshop leaders who teach us about spiritual direction, and as I practice my own teaching skills.

Christ is a compassionate teacher, respecting our deepest integrity as individuals. Not seductive, but delighting in us. Not promoting a hidden agenda, but teaching us the way to listen. Not softening our resolve with false promises and self-serving kindness, but asking us to surrender into joy. I say this from experience, because I still doubt anything I can't feel in my bones, can't locate in the deepest center of my heart. I don't trust anyone just because they stand up in front of a classroom or in front of a congregation. In fact, I may trust them less. I don't hand over my loyalty lightly, and my restlessness has kept me moving, looking for the Infallible Teacher, who is Christ.

Redemption
A Song and a Prayer

Through all the tumult and the strife
I hear the music ringing;
It finds an echo in my soul—
How can I keep from singing?

—Protestant hymn,
Robert Lowry, 1860

Lectio Divina is a contemplative prayer practice currently very popular with Christian spiritual directors and retreat leaders, in which a portion of scripture is used as a means of entering into the *stories* of Christ and God's interaction with humanity through prayerful and imaginative reflection. First, a scripture passage is chosen. Often the passage is selected because of some particular theme or image that feels pertinent to the present moment, or because it seems to relate to some significant point on the spiritual journey. People who embrace the practice of Lectio Divina speak of the powerful experience of entering into a participatory relationship with all aspects of the story. So far, in my encounters with this form of prayer in a group situation I have remained unmoved, probably due to my tendency to resist being *told* what passage to read and reflect upon, with the attendant assumption that I will be moved by it. Recently, when I have attempted to enter more deeply into a chosen passage of scripture on my own, I have had more success.

During one of my spiritual direction workshops this spring, we were asked to practice Lectio Divina using a reading from 1 Samuel 3:1–10. The workshop leader suggested we relax into a meditative posture, put our books and papers on the floor, and settle ourselves comfortably in our chairs. Lectio Divina and indeed, much of spiritual direction practice, is about *noticing,* a favorite word in our training. It signals a focused desire to pay attention to inner movements of the heart and spirit. She explained that the passage would be read through three times. The first time through, we were to focus on noticing our general responses to the story. Did we sense any inner stirrings, any inner movement, either toward or away from the story? Did we enter into the story as Samuel, or Eli, or even as God, calling us by name? After a few moments of silence, she would read through the passage again. This time we were to pay attention to any place in the story where we felt particularly stirred by an image or a word or a phrase. Then, after yet some more silence, we would listen to it a third time through to deepen our awareness of our inner stirring, where we had been drawn into the Word.

I closed my eyes and at first, all I noticed was how tired I was. My back hurt, and I could feel a cold settling in my head and chest. I felt doubtful, but ready to try. She began to read.

"During the time young Samuel was minister to the Lord under Eli, a revelation of the Lord was uncommon and visions, infrequent."

So far so good; the passage had my attention. I have always liked this scripture reading, and the particular translation she had chosen to read from was elegantly written. After being distracted by thinking about the vagaries of biblical translation, I focused again on the present moment. As she read on, however, I noticed only the tenor of her voice, a misplaced inflection here and there,

45

a word I would have replaced with another. The story of Samuel being called by God usually resonates with me, but tonight I only hear it. I don't actually *feel* it. Maybe it's because I'm a writer, maybe it's because I am not facile at shifting my attention from a group dynamic to a private listening, but this form of prayer on this particular night doesn't work for me. I hear the words, notice the language used, the imagery chosen, and I stay on the surface of the experience. Maybe I don't like being told I will now have a moving experience, an encounter on demand. Fortunately for me, when we meet with a partner afterward to share our experience, she has a similar reaction. We talk instead about what does work for us and move on into the rest of the evening.

I wanted to get from here to there, from the inland lake of my own experience to the great ocean of spirit and life beyond.

On the way home that night, I thought again about this prayer practice, so central to much of Christian spirituality. Why didn't it work for me? I wondered as I drove along the freeway in the rain and the dark. Did I not give it enough of a chance? Did I resist it because I wasn't in control of what I would hear? What if I chose the passage myself, at home — would that work? Tired of pondering, I turned on the car's CD player. The only CD available belonged to my daughter: Bob Marley and the Wailers. I remembered one track she had played recently that was new to me: "Redemption Song." Though Marley was very popular during my teenage years, I certainly never heard this song at any high-school party back in the seventies. A plaintive guitar and then Bob Marley's voice filled the car, and I entered into the song.

When I was a child and a teenager, music was my form of Lectio Divina. I would play album tracks over and over, memorizing each word, each inflection, each rhythm change until I could mimic the singer without a misstep. A song such as "A Case of You," by Joni Mitchell, could hold my attention for hours, and still does now, twenty-five years later. Thinking about those days, I tried listening to this song this morning. I could barely stay with it as all the heartache of being seventeen flooded back in a moment. In those days, I wanted to "be" the song even more than I wanted to be the singer. In order to enter into a song like that I would try to sing just like the singer, copying her style, her tone, her breathing. At some point when I knew the song so well I could play it through in my mind as vividly as if it were playing out loud, it became my song.

But there was nothing beyond my song to hold on to, nothing but an accumulated weight of memory. The problem with love songs, I have found, especially back when I was a teenager, is that any effects such as feeling comforted or understood or immersed in love and longing only last as long as the song itself lasts: Beyond that I couldn't use it to transcend my own pain, or my own immediate experience. A love song could take me on a journey into my feelings but not help me merge into communion with anything greater than my own private world of emotional angst. I left the Lectio Divina practice of popular music behind when I decided to stop wading in the small pool of my own desire. I wanted to get from here to there, from the inland lake of my own experience to the great ocean of spirit and life beyond. At the time, I didn't know how to get there, and love songs weren't the way.

Now, driving home after the workshop all these years later, I found myself drawn to a song with a desire I didn't understand but was willing to surrender to. I played "Redemption Song" in the car the next day as I chauffeured kids around and ran errands. I sat in my driveway after I had parked, and played it again. And again. The reggae rhythms were unfamiliar to me at first, so it took several more listenings all day as I tentatively sang along to get even the basics of inflection and syncopation. I submerged myself in the dialect, in the casual grammar, and let my rusty voice warm to the rounded tones. The song is about freedom, and God, and redemption, and community. It's about love, but not love as a one-way street toward thwarted desire, or waiting for someone who never arrives. As I listened and opened my heart to the music, I didn't think about how I might be practicing a form of Lectio Divina. It felt more like playing, like dancing, like youth revisited, like magic. As the war news about Iraq worsened on the radio and the TV that day, I hummed this song under my breath, entering into the comfort and truth of it, and exchanged my own immediate reality for a larger wisdom. Because of this, I think I now better understand the mechanism and the mystery of "engaging the text" as they say in spiritual direction circles, although I didn't consciously engage the text that day, not really; Bob Marley engaged me, I responded, and Christ was there.

"Because the Bible Tells Me So..."

Three of the spiritual directors I have worked with are nuns. They have a casual yet profound acquaintance with scripture in a way I can only hope to emulate. I still let myself get sidetracked by the irrelevancies that ultimately don't do anything besides provide an excuse for staying out of its depths altogether. Which translation is best and how much is "historical" truth versus "poetic" truth; issues of gendered language and textual manipulations and inaccurate interpretations of complex metaphor — who cares? I know, we all care, but to what degree? I can study and argue with myself and skip from the NIV to the KJV, but it's all fancy footwork. After all is said and done, I still must open the Bible and read, immerse myself in the story, open my mind and heart. This is how I have adapted the Lectio Divina practice to my own needs.

The passage that most intrigues me these days is John 8:6, where Jesus is bent down, drawing in the dirt. I wonder to myself, "What is he doing? What is he thinking as people gather around, arguing and trying to draw him in to their crisis?" But mostly I don't try to winnow out his thoughts.

I can study and argue with myself and skip from the NIV to the KJV, but it's all fancy footwork. After all is said and done, I still must open the Bible and read, immerse myself in the story, open my mind and heart.

I just carry around this image of Christ as I shop for groceries, walk on the beach, and drive in my car. Here I am, doing these things, and there he is, drawing in the dirt. I long to wander over and kneel down beside him, look up into his face, be near him in silence.

For me as a Christian spiritual director, the Bible is available as another window into God, like prayer and ritual and communal worship. In my training program, which is founded on Christian principles, we talk about scripture much less than one might expect. After all, we have rabbis and Muslims in our group as well, and our essential call is to respond to God, not to respond to Christianity, though I imagine it's assumed that we all diligently pursue the study of whatever texts most inform our own tradition. So I could give the Bible short shrift if I wanted to. Who would notice? And sometimes I am tempted, given how infuriating and labyrinthine it can be, and yet it is the written document of Christ, and so I struggle on, finding both rocky ground and everlasting springs for my trouble.

Who Am I to Talk?

Let the words of my mouth, and the meditation of my heart be acceptable to you, O Lord, my rock and my redeemer.

—Psalm 19:14

One of the things I have struggled most with during my spiritual direction training concerns knowing when to talk and when to keep quiet. It's not that I'm not listening when other people share; rather I am listening intently, and from that intense engagement with what they are sharing I want to contribute my own thoughts and feelings that have been stirred up by what they said. I am so eager for interaction, so hungry for authentic expression and communication. I also think a lot, and it's nice to share what I think. As a writer who works alone, I'm happy for the opportunity to give and get immediate feedback. So when I start wondering if I am talking too much, it's not usually because I actually feel that way myself, but because I wonder if other people feel that way. I become self-conscious and doubt myself.

At lunch I sat with Joyce, and we talked how the month had gone in our respective lives, and we talked about talking. "I worry that I talk too much in this group," she said. Joyce is a psychotherapist and eloquently conveys her thoughts and experiences in our workshops. I always like hearing what she has to say. I told her how much I liked to listen to her, and yet I understood her feeling.

"Me too," I confessed, "though I talk anyway." We agreed that we operate from a past history of feeling as though we should defer to others and not dominate any discussion or any interaction. Later that day as I drove home, I reviewed the workshop in my mind and wondered again if I had talked too much. Did I prevent others from speaking by filling the gap before they could summon up the courage to jump in? Did I allow myself to sit in silence long enough to pay attention to what I really felt? Or to look at it more positively, did I speak from a knowledge and enthusiasm of the subject, generating discussion and insights, adding to the discussion in a fruitful way?

As spiritual directors in direct communion with our directees, we are encouraged not to talk, but to listen and to notice. Not just to the other person, but for the stirrings, images, physical sensations, and intuitive responses in ourselves that signal the presence of God. We move toward a contemplative stance. When I am formulating what I am going to say next without paying attention on these other levels, I am all mind. I am operating only from one aspect of my humanness, open to only one aspect of the spirit. It's not as though we mimic the stereotype of a psychiatrist, nodding for an hour and saying nothing but "What do you think it means?" in a passive way. But speaking from a place grounded in an awareness of the Spirit is different from talking in order to hold someone's attention or to force a point of view. We practice this kind of awareness a lot, and it has helped me to notice my eagerness when I am excited about what someone is saying. Not only in spiritual direction, but in everyday interactions. Finding the balance between not stifling my voice and allowing room for the voices of others and of God, will be, I imagine, a lifetime practice.

Trusting the Teacher

More about Jesus let me learn,
More of His holy will discern;
Spirit of God, my teacher be,
Showing the things of Christ to me.

—"More About Jesus,"
Eliza E. Hewitt, 1887

One regular Wednesday evening after a dinner of take-out pizza and homemade salad and while the kids were settled at their homework, I asked my husband if he'd had a chance to read any part of the book I'd left on his desk. The book, written by a Buddhist nun, had affected my spiritual equilibrium, such as it was. In fact, I'd cried while reading it the prior week. Normally, the only creative art that makes me cry is music. I'm often moved to tears by a singer's ability to weave through a song like a bird hovering on the wind. Only last Sunday I'd become tearful when the church soloist held a sustained note near the end of the "Alleluia." With this book, however, I wasn't sure what had made me cry.

I admit I rather cornered my husband, who I suspect wanted to watch the History Channel and eat his dessert. I wanted his input as an ex-Catholic seminarian who regularly practices the tenets of Buddhism and meditates. I wanted to know what he thought about the dichotomy I felt between the way I respond internally when I read books on Buddhism, and my own experience of the mystery of Christ. I wanted to talk. Andy's an obliging sort, so he listened.

I started by pointing out that I have no problem with the Buddhist concept of impermanence and change. I understand and accept that suffering often arises from trying to hold on to some semblance of stability and permanence. After all, I've been married more than once, and I've moved over twenty-five times in forty-three years. "Everything changes, nothing stays the same" is more than a cliché for me: it's been a mantra that has helped me though many transitions and stuck places. In fact, if anything, I have the opposite problem. It's been hard for me to embrace anything fully except my own restlessness. My husband nodded as I talked. I paused while I thought about what is constant for me: my love for my children and my love for this man waiting so patiently and nonjudgmentally for me to work out my anxiety by talking. While he listened and ate his brownies and ice cream, I tried to articulate how empty the book made me feel as I read each chapter. The author's words made perfect sense to me from an intellectual perspective, but they did not resonate in my heart. Was I missing the point? Had I not read enough about Buddhism to really *get* it?

"Buddhism is a very complicated philosophy, with many different strains practiced here and around the world," my husband pointed out, setting aside his empty dessert dish. "Some practice very devotionally, while others are more grounded in the mind. It's a lifelong journey with many paths. You may not have found the approach that works for you."

I thought about that, and wondered, briefly, if it was true. Was it just a matter of finding a form of Buddhism that worked best for me? I was tempted to steer the topic into a fascinating discussion about the various schools of Buddhism and the implications for

Western practitioners, but that would have been stalling. I cut to the chase.

"When I think about or try to *feel* my way into Buddhism, it feels constricting to me. When I approach Christianity with my mind and heart, it feels expansive."

"I understand what you are saying," he said. "But the opposite is true for me."

We smiled at each other and sat in silence for a few moments. Yet I still had more I needed to talk about.

> I understand and accept that suffering often arises from trying to hold on to some semblance of stability and permanence.... "Everything changes, nothing stays the same" is more than a cliché for me: it's been a mantra that has helped me though many transitions and stuck places.

"Here's the part that made me cry. It's near the end of the book. She talks about finding a teacher. How she found this teacher, even though she felt fearful and unsure, and wondered at her sense of being so drawn to this teacher. She knew that she needed to surrender herself, to make a full commitment to the relationship in order to grow spiritually. She said that her teacher is her connection to the sacred." I paused. My husband must have sensed how emotional this made me feel, even if he didn't know why.

"Well, that's a very common practice in some forms of Buddhism: finding a teacher who embodies the Buddha," he offered.

"I could never surrender to another human being like that," I said. "I don't believe in that. I don't even like having my faith experience affected by whether the preaching was good or bad on Sunday, never mind giving over my power to some person who will direct my whole spiritual experience." My husband nodded. I knew he felt the same way. Meanwhile I noticed that our children had drifted into the room and had draped themselves over chairs and on the bed, listening quietly. I kept on, determined to get to the heart of what I needed to say.

"Yet I understand and believe in the importance of commitment. I think when my heart starts pounding in church sometimes it's a call toward commitment. I don't like this book's emphasis on impermanence, because it's too easy for me to use the reality of physical impermanence to justify not committing fully to God. It's easy for me to see all things as fluid and changing, so why ground myself in God? But I had a thought."

I hesitated, unsure of how he would receive this next revelation of mine, realizing even as I hesitated, how important his response would be to me. Amazingly, our kids didn't interrupt. Maybe they sensed my struggle. I had no idea what he would say, since this was new territory for me.

"Instead of a person, what if I were to approach Christ as my teacher? Do you think that could work? Or do you think that's nuts?"

"Absolutely that would work," he said emphatically. He went on to say that he believes that Christ is a living and present reality that we can experience, and a teacher well worth committing to and learning from in order to experience God. Not the only teacher, he added from his ecumenical stance, but a powerful one.

My husband is a very practical man. He has no agenda, as far as I have been able to tell in six years of marriage, regarding what he wants or expects for me (or anyone) spiritually. When he does his work as a hospice nurse, he is grounded in the immediate reality of pain and suffering, not worrying about abstract concepts about teachers. When I talk with the spiritual directors I know who are also nuns, I find it easy to say to myself as they talk about Christ, "Of course you believe that. You're a nun." In this way I can try to rationalize what they say about the living presence of Christ. But Andy? A man who lives in the technical world of computers during the week and gives practical advice, compassion, and nursing care to the dying and their families on weekends? A man who doesn't go to Mass with us except on special occasions, who left seminary after two years? No agenda.

Then the phone rang and our daughter needed help with her homework and I had to make a trip to the grocery store for something or other, and the moment passed, but I kept that possibility very close to my heart. Christ, my teacher. Hmmm.

The Holy Longing
The Search for a Christian Spirituality
by Ron Rolheiser

I have always been a voracious reader, and these last few years of reading books about Christ, Christianity, and spirituality have been no exception (balanced by the two or three mystery novels I read each week and numerous religious magazines). Usually I find these religious books thought provoking, sometimes boring, less often irritating. One book which moved beyond piquing my intellectual interest into a genuine resonance with my spiritual experience is *The Holy Longing:*

The Search for a Christian Spirituality by Ronald Rolheiser, O.M.I. Our local Catholic paper carries a column by Rolheiser, and reading it drew me to look for his books, because his columns challenged me to think more clearly, invited me into prayer, and consoled me with their companionable tone. *The Holy Longing* opens this way: "This is a book for you if you are struggling spiritually." He then goes on to articulate the framework of Christian spirituality in ways that helped me envision my faith as a living structure I could venture into and find Christ, as grand as a cathedral, as creative as the Watts Towers, welcoming as a garden, awesome as the wilderness. As a restless Christian I want to hear about how I can approach and embrace Christian spirituality, not be inundated with religious doctrine. Rolheiser manages an amalgamation of both that is flexible yet firm, committed yet not rigid. Not every book comes into my life at the right time, but this one showed up when I needed it, and I have revisited it often since then. I've suggested it to a couple of my directees when they asked about books I would recommend, but I have to be careful not to wax too enthusiastic or to make it seem like something I am requiring them to read. I'm not in charge of their theological training, and if they don't like the book they might feel awkward saying so. I rarely respond very well to a book that I have been "told" to read. Being a rebellious sort, I prefer to think I've gone my own way, found my own source, forged my own path. What an illusion!

As a Restless Child

Then little children were being brought to him in order that he might lay his hands on them and pray. The disciples spoke sternly to those who brought them; But Jesus said, Let the little children come to me, and do not stop them; for it is to such as these that the kingdom of heaven belongs.

—Matthew 19:13–14

I volunteer in my children's elementary school as a facilitator for a group of kids who have experienced a divorce or death in their families. As part of my training I received a detailed manual with suggested exercises for each week including art projects, talking points, and general themes. After the second week I realized that the manual was only going to take me so far: the rest was up to me. Working with my small group of fourth and fifth graders, I was struck by how willing they were to make eye contact. One little girl always rushed to sit next to me and indeed often leaned up against me, hugging me and whispering in my ear. Another boy offered me some of his lunch each week, which I politely declined. They were upset the one day I was five minutes late because they needed to be able to rely on me to be consistent, something often lacking in divorced families. They also wanted me to listen to each one of them exclusively, often patting my hand or tapping my shoulder to get my attention when I talked to another child for too long. Each child coped with a similar set of circumstances at home. All came from single-parent families, and most had learned to deal with such stressors as visitation schedules and arguing parents, either in person or over the phone. And they all shared a similar life experience: the precariousness of adult attention, and the fragility of love. I had expected to have to work to get these kids to trust me, to open up, to talk. Yet trust and sharing weren't the issues at all. Instead, the main thing that characterized our meetings was their inability to focus.

Children are the personification of restlessness. If they are too acquiescent or passive I begin to wonder what might be wrong. I am reassured by restless energy, a waving about of arms, tapping feet, bursts of laughter, lots of questions. Even if a child is naturally quiet by nature, there is usually some spark, something propelling them forward into life, even if it's mainly occurring in their heads.

My husband and I are raising a child who has always had trouble focusing on anything he wasn't intensely interested in. Now, at fourteen, our son's ability to pay attention, concentrate, and stay focused has merged with his ability to learn and his own innate intelligence, and it's as if the kaleidoscope of who he is has moved into a cohesive and comprehensive pattern. The disparate elements of his energy and intelligence and imagination have connected and are synchronized, and he's becoming his own person, a centered, stable, creative, and interesting young man. Because he has now learned how to focus and pay attention on his own, he trusts his own abilities more, and trusts that he will succeed, which in turn means that he usually does succeed.

What if I had given up on him at age five, or seven, or twelve, too impatient with his abstracted attention and too angry at his seeming indifference? What if I had decided that this restless, high-strung, absent-minded child was deliberately wandering from the point, or choosing to stray from the path that his parents and his teachers so clearly and carefully laid out? I needed to offer an unvarying stream of love and attention, without judgment or second-guessing my decision to do so. Because I am not Christ, I sometimes failed at this, and lost my temper or despaired. But always I returned to loving him, to focusing my attention.

So spending an hour a week with five children who wandered around the room, changed the subject repeatedly, interrupted each other, grabbed each other's food, and generally ignored the lesson plan didn't faze me, at least not too much. Bit by bit, I got their attention. I kept my message simple: I am here to listen. I kept my voice even, my gaze on them loving and constant, and I waited for any opening in the conversation, any indication that they might be ready to hear what I had to offer, or might be willing to go a little more bravely into their feelings. And briefly, in flashes, they focused, we connected, and it seemed like some healing took place.

Children are the personification of restlessness. If they are too acquiescent or passive I begin to wonder what might be wrong. I am reassured by restless energy, a waving about of arms, tapping feet, bursts of laughter, lots of questions. Even if a child is naturally quiet by nature, there is usually some spark, something propelling them forward into life, even if it's mainly occurring in their heads. What they seem to want, at least from me, at least the children I have raised or worked with or just known and loved, is constant attention. Not an obsessive, intrusive gaze or nosy interaction, but a feeling that we are always immediately available when needed. One little boy in my group needed me from the beginning of the hour until the end, and he had no problem letting me know it. He tried to convince the other kids they would have more fun outside, because he wanted me all to himself. Another child hardly noticed me at all, until the week I returned after having been sick the week before. She was very angry with me for the first half hour and ignored me, then she handed me a crayon drawing on her way out that had a large picture of a smiling girl and the words, "Glad yer back."

I see myself in these children, in my relationship to Christ. I've also craved attention and love from people who were inconsistent and unreliable and inattentive. This makes it hard for me as an adult to trust the constancy of Christ. Like a child, I get angry if I believe that Christ has gone away. I crave being close to Christ, warmed by his presence, and like a young child, I get jealous of others who seem to be in closer relationship to Christ than I am. Yet I have also learned, in my own effective response to a child's restlessness, how Christ might respond to me if I can only focus long enough to take it in. Perhaps Christ will be patient with me as I was patient with my son, as I grow into my own sense of self and learn to trust my ability to pay attention, to love, to succeed. Christ's voice is even, his gaze is constant. I know this because my ability to be present to others is imbued with Christ's presence. It must be so, because in my relationships I am often more patient, more loving, more attentive, more focused than I believe I am capable of on my own: Christ manifests all of these things *through* me. As I learn how to pay attention to children and to everyone including my directees, I begin to wonder: perhaps Christ's attentiveness is an even greater and limitless presence than mine is for my own children. If my attention and love can help bring about such healing and growth and transformation on a relatively small scale, what might happen in my own life, if I could allow Christ to reach me in my own restlessness, if I could only pay enough attention?

Christin the Margins

*I believe that I shall see the goodness of the Lord
in the land of the living.* —Psalm 27:13

Last week in our spiritual direction workshop the topic was marginalization, as experienced by our directees and ourselves. It's
too large a subject to be covered in a graduate program, never
mind a one-day workshop, but we did our best. What does being
marginalized mean in this context? I thought to myself, looking
around the room. We are a group mainly composed of middle-
class white women (and two men). We don't fit the political
definition of marginalized people, which mostly classifies people
as marginalized based on the criteria of economics, ethnicity, disability, or race. Marginalized people in a political context are those
people who don't fit the "norms" of the dominant culture they
live in. In our spiritual direction group, we aren't suffering un-
duly from poverty or racism or discrimination, at least not in the
political sense, at least not overtly, here in the relatively liberal
San Francisco Bay Area. It's true that there are a few gay and lesbian people among us who are marginalized by the mainstream,
heterosexual culture and have no doubt experienced discrimination based on their sexual identity. A small handful of us are not
European American and have known a degree and type of discrimination in our American society that the European Americans
haven't. Some are Jewish and one is Sufi-Muslim, which may or

may not be problematic in American culture these days, depending on the milieu they operate within. Overall, however, we are a privileged group in global, political terms: well educated, well employed, well housed, and well fed. We may, because of our general outlook and values, feel alienated from the larger society, but that is more of a psychological or even spiritual condition rather than a political or cultural reality.

I thought about that as we discussed marginalization. In my graduate program in education, this topic served as the foundation for studying the trends and forces in higher education. I have had some personal, albeit minor, experience with it as well. But, as someone asked in the workshop, how do we define marginalization? Does it encompass not only culture, economics, politics, and race, but spirituality as well? Although many of us self-identify as Christians, a dominant tradition in our culture, we often feel marginalized within our faith tradition as we adhere to a different set of values based on authentic spiritual experience rather than the rules and pronouncements of our various denominations. Overall, we agreed that if we could understand both our own experiences of marginalization and the marginalization that others have suffered from in whatever guise, we might better be able to respond to this dimension in our own and our directees' lives.

We gathered mid-morning into small groups, after spending some time writing about any personal experience we could recall of feeling marginalized. It came to me as we shared our experiences in turn, that except for the gay and lesbian folks or the non-European Americans among us, there was a distinct element of choice in our marginalized situations. Unless we are someone born into dire poverty or into a skin color, sexual preference, or disability that automatically places us on the margins of our dominant culture, we had and continue to have options about our marginalized status. We have chosen the relationship, the career, the educational path, the faith tradition, or the cultural milieu that subsequently causes us to feel set apart. We might feel marginalized because we don't fit the ideal model of a successful person in our culture: married, raising children, college educated, only in relationships with other "successful" people like us, living out the lifestyle of the "American Dream." Yet some of these differences from the norm can be modified, albeit at the risk of denying our own personal identity. A single person can marry. Careers can be changed, education obtained, relationships ended, cultural norms assimilated. Even a faith tradition can be chosen or changed, though some would argue that our call from God is not truly a choice, unless we choose to ignore it.

Although many of us self-identify as Christians, a dominant tradition in our culture, we often feel marginalized within our faith tradition as we adhere to a different set of values based on authentic spiritual experience rather than the rules and pronouncements of our various denominations.

Still, despite differences in the degree and type of marginalization we had all known, the experiences we shared that day were real, the feelings intense. Our experiences mostly centered on a sense of displacement, of not feeling connected to the consumerist, media-centered culture we found ourselves in. All in all, we were united by our shared awareness of not fully adhering to a designated role in some way, whether in our careers, relationships, or culture. In some aspect of our identity, we don't feel as if we "fit," at least not all the time.

Over lunch, my friend Joyce and I talked about marginalization. Joyce is white, and her partner is African American. We agreed that even though she and I may feel marginalized because of our personal perspectives about our culture, we can "pass" in most any social or work situation if we choose to do so. We are well-spoken and presentable in terms of what our corporate and educational culture expects, and would be welcomed in nearly every classroom, every boardroom, every social milieu favored by our white, secular, well-off American culture. Unlike someone who is African American, Joyce pointed out, who can't pretend to be any other race, she and I can choose to go along to get along, although there is a price to pay in terms of being true to our authentic selves.

After lunch, as we gathered together again, someone suggested that we are all marginalized as people choosing to seek a spiritual path. She meant that our secularized and materialized culture does not favor people who choose to spend a sunny Saturday praying together and talking about the call of the Holy Spirit. So be it. Could any of us, once awakened to the stirrings of the mystery, return to a blind acceptance of the secular status quo? Could we quell our longing hearts, subdue our restless spirits? As I move more steadily into the core of what it means to be a spiritual director, I realize I have chosen a radical stance in our secular culture that I can't easily back out of, and that I can't rest content with "passing" as someone who isn't committed to a path toward Christ. Nor do I want to. I may even encounter discrimination from those who have a preconceived and negative notion of what it means to be Christian and will judge me accordingly.

"The margins are an open doorway into a connection with God," I offered later that day. And I thought to myself, as we continued to share our stories of feeling marginalized, separate, and awakened from the norm, that Christ chose to live in the margins. I can't truly know what it means to suffer from racial or sexual discrimination, and can't fully enter into the experience of being marginalized by our culture for being disabled, or homeless, or mentally ill. I can only hope to emulate his actions and his love in my own small way.

Romancing Christ

For wisdom is better than jewels,
and all that you desire cannot compare with her.
—Proverbs 8:11

Several years ago, in the midst of a troubled marriage that had me feeling trapped with no way out that I could think of, my mother and I escaped the Bay Area and took the kids on a day trip to the small town of Sonoma, California. The day was hot, the vineyards and fields we passed on the way were heavy with scent, and the children were willing to be humored with the promise of lunch and playtime in the grassy square in the center of town. We strolled around the square peering into antique shops, cheese and wine shops, and bookstores. One window in particular caught my eye. A combination bookstore and purveyor of all things New Age, the window held crystals and dragon figurines, candles and beads. I was enchanted by the colors and whimsy, and felt a longing straight to my heart for magic, for a life painted in purple and gold and wrapped in silk and velvet. I wanted to wear jewels and long flowing clothes. I longed to step into another world, one not burdened by worries about relationships, petty fights, and anxiety. I didn't buy anything in the store that day, partly from lack of money (why are the accoutrements of the New Age so expensive?) and partly because my Protestant suspicion of icons, images, and just plain "stuff" as irrelevant distractions from God at best or idolatry at worst held me back.

I wanted so much to surround myself with the *things* that represent the lore of mystery and magic and romance. I wanted to own them so they could somehow transform my life. I guess I hoped that if I lit candles, played a CD of medieval music, burned some sage incense, and arranged crystals, stones, and flowers on a self-designed altar that my life might then become something more poetic, more meaningful. I wanted to enter into the realm of knighthood and quests and deep woods, a world of dappled sunlight and wine, honor and spells. I am attracted to these symbols of a long-ago time, even if it only exists or has ever existed in books. I can transport myself there readily in books of fantasy fiction, but I have never found the alchemical formula which will transform these symbols of mystery from objects that exist outside of myself into a world where I move and breathe and find my being.

I have come to discover that while stones, rivers, trees, flowers, and wilderness places embody the divine, they are not ultimately a replacement for direct engagement with Christ.

Ron Rolheiser, in a column on June 1, 2003, titled, "Vocations: Where Has the Romance Gone" in *Catholic San Francisco,* argued that the romantic imagination must be engaged in order to sustain a lasting commitment to the challenges of religious vocation. The Catholic Church, I have always thought, excels at romance. Clothed in saints and icons and incense, it offers a rich ambience that a Protestant church such as my father preached in, with its plain glass windows and no altar, lacked. Yet perhaps because I am not a born-into-the-church Catholic, the trappings of church don't have the same effect on me. I am no more transformed by lighting a candle in the sanctuary than I am by lighting a candle on a rock in the woods at winter solstice. That is, I am not transformed by a ritual or its symbols or tools unless God is present in my heart, and no beautiful icon or labyrinth walk can create that connection in and of itself. The romance I seek as a part of my relationship with Christ doesn't exist anywhere outside of myself: not even, ultimately, in nature.

Even more than in candles and dragons and crystal necklaces, I have looked for God in the romantic setting of the wilderness. Yet I have come to discover that while stones, rivers, trees, flowers, and wilderness places embody the divine, they are not ultimately a replacement for direct engagement with Christ. Rather, they are the setting for Christ; a manifestation of Mystery, but not Mystery. Inanimate objects placed at the center of my deep need offer me nothing but loneliness. Wilderness at the center of my longing offers me only more longing. Given only dragons and romantic rituals as food for my soul, I remain hungry for more, restless for adventure, for connection, for Christ. I need more than symbols and icons, more than beauty and poetry, though these things can, sometimes, serve as intimations of God. They can be fun, charming, comforting, playful, and attractive. Yet I'd rather skip the froufrou and go straight to the source, the true romance of loving Christ and receiving Wisdom. There is mystery there, in abundance, enough to satisfy the most poetic imagination, the most creative spirit.

Call and Response

Christ didn't redeem us by a direct intellectual act, but became incarnate in human form, and he speaks to us now through the mediation of a visible Church.

—Flannery O'Connor, *Mystery and Manners*

"Who am I to write about this?" is a concern that comes up a lot when I work with writers who want to write about spirituality. Americans are very concerned with what "right" one has to say anything; we want to know a person's credentials first before we agree to consider what he or she is saying. In the wonderful collection of Quaker writings edited by J. Brent Bill, *Imagination and Spirit,* the first essay by Thomas Kelly, on "holy obedience," refers to the need for humility. He counsels against comparing ourselves to others in terms of worldly achievements, because our worth is truly and only measured in God's sight. Yet the introduction to the very next essay focuses on the worldly achievements of the author (in this case, Elton Trueblood) as a professor and writer, noting his professional degrees and accomplishments as something impressive. Many people want to be taken seriously as writers, speakers, or retreat leaders (and usually all three) who are allowed to participate in the larger cultural conversation about faith. As religious intellectuals, spiritual mentors, and creative people, we exist on two planes as created by our culture. There is the private realm of true relationship to Christ and to God which requires nothing but our full, intimate participation and trust in a call and response, and the reality of our intellectual and professional achievements as religious intellectuals, spiritual mentors, and creative people which, if we want to reach people beyond our immediate circle, requires that we publish, give speeches, win honors, and publicize ourselves as experts speaking to laypeople. Religious literature assures us that spiritual wisdom doesn't depend on worldly status and accomplishment, though these are sometimes tools for disseminating wisdom. And surely all the worldly accomplishments and status that one can accrue in one lifetime won't lead to spiritual wisdom without first being grounded in a heartfelt and spirit-centered experience that requires no Ph.D., no salary, no name recognition, but only an interactive love affair with God.

We have developed a cultural system of determining who to recognize and give accolades to for several reasons. In practical terms, unless we are supported by a religious order or come from wealth, we all need to earn a living. How do we raise our voice above the crowded marketplace? With the megaphone of marketing departments and larger venues and from the platforms of tenure, the pulpit, or the media. This is not necessarily a bad thing, because an essential aspect of the creative energy that flows through us all is the desire to share our spiritual wisdom and creativity with others. Because the marketplace is crowded, because we have been deceived in the past, because we no longer believe everything we hear from our leaders, we seek other ways to determine whether we should pay attention to a particular voice.

Who do I trust to speak to me, to teach me about God? I approach the message of designated religious experts warily. Instead of automatically admiring them, I usually mistrust them on principle. I'm about as untrusting as it gets when it comes to accepting the word of any institution or designated leader as being the

73

"truth." Nothing makes me more restless than being told something that I am supposed to accept simply because of the status of the speaker. This has even been true for me when reading the Bible. I have resisted taking anyone else's word for it that the Bible is Truth with a capital T. My first reaction has always been, Who says? When there is no call and response in learning or in faith, just a lecture or a "because I said so" attitude, then I shut down, clam up like a stubborn child, and resist. I want to participate, I want hands-on faith, and my restlessness in the face of someone talking at me instead of with me keeps me searching for more.

What I have realized over the course of my faith journey is that I have come to an intellectual understanding and belief about my faith only when I have first of all *felt* God's mystery. Then and only then can that experience be grounded by intellectual exploration and a thoughtful, reasoned acceptance of what it means for me in terms of my understanding of faith and Christ. I reject theories and doctrine that don't square with what I have *felt* to be true. The body of spiritual and religious literature available has often helped me recognize those times when I have experienced God's presence and not understood what it meant for me in terms of faith, direction, and meaning. I have those wonderful "Aha" moments that feel like I am in a conversation with the writer or the teacher. Yet there have been times when I didn't understand something I had read or been told because I hadn't *lived* it yet. For example, I had read and been preached to for years about forgiving those who hurt us, but I could not truly understand the implications for my faith, or experience a true conversion of heart until I forgave someone who had radically hurt me. The gift of forgiveness came from my relationship with Christ, not from reading about what Christ had to say about forgiveness. All the reading or preaching in the world couldn't convert my anger into forgiveness. That came through Christ's love. Yet after I had forgiven someone, I could return to Christ's words on forgiveness with a closer understanding of what he meant. My spiritual restlessness and resistance to worldly assurances of "how it works" eventually led me to try trusting the very source of spiritual wisdom, Christ. In this way I bypassed all others, only returning to the writers and theologians and other wisdom teachers when I felt I could rely on my own felt experience of Christ enough to discern the truth of what they have to impart.

You see, reading about faith, Christianity, or Christ, or hearing people preach about them has never been enough to convince me, at a core level, of anything. In fact, attempts to do so by religion writers have usually left me quite skeptical, even when I really wanted to believe what they were telling me. I have responded best when I have recognized in someone else's story or discourse what I have already known to be true but had not previously articulated. I have left myself open to other possibilities by also reading and experiencing the tenets of many other faiths, from Buddhism to Wicca, so that I could be sure I had not closed any doors out of ignorance. The reason I now embrace a faith path that centers on Christ is that it makes sense to me on every level of my being, from emotional to intellectual, and yet the primary touchstone for me as to whether or not this path is the right one for me, despite all intellectual arguments, remains, "Have I felt this to be true?"

I believe I have had these felt experiences not only because I "chose" to have them, but because I was called to have them by the living Christ. I had to be willing enough or desperate enough to accept whatever outcome might arise from my humble prayer, "Thy will be done." No worldly knowledge of mine or of anyone else's, no Ph.D. or publishing history, no amount of books or study or writing, can replace that direct call and response.

Committed to the Journey

The term spiritual director is a misnomer is some ways; it implies that someone will be telling you how to organize and practice your spiritual life. Actually, a spiritual director helps you listen to the Spirit by listening to and with you and helping you learn to observe how God is at work in your life.

—Debra Farrington, *Hearing with the Heart:*
A Gentle Guide to Discerning God's Will for Your Life

A couple of weeks after the last workshop for year two of the training, I met with a supervisor from year three for an interview. The trees around Mercy Center basked in the late May sunlight, and I could see someone walking the labyrinth path as I made my way to the main building. We'd been asked to write our responses to some interview questions, and I'd worked on them the day before. The questions ranged from the practical: would I be able to find three to five directees to meet with starting in September? (Yes.) To the more mystical: how do I continue to feel called to the ministry of spiritual direction?

Although I spent some thoughtful time answering the questions in writing, I approached the interview feeling open to whatever might arise in our conversation. Mentally rehearsed meetings make me nervous. I much prefer the improvisational, as long as I've done my homework. During my Al-Anon years, when asked to speak at meetings, I wouldn't mentally prepare a topic or plan how to frame my story in advance. I'd just offer up a prayer for holy wisdom before opening my mouth and take it from there, which seemed to generate the most positive response. I suspect that I'm subconsciously discerning and analyzing and conversing with myself and with God all the time anyway; sometimes I just continue this conversation out loud, with the added benefit of another person's input and attention. I try my best to pay attention in return.

Ever since adolescence, my spiritual restlessness has compelled me to look for a path, a framework, a way of life that I could commit to. I tried the way of the artist, the intellectual, the hedonist, the rebel, the homemaker, the mother, the wife, the church community member. . . . I have ended up being all of these things to some degree at one time or another, and none of these things to a complete degree, not to the very depths of my soul.

One of the questions we discussed that day in the interview had to do with being called. In what ways do I notice whether I am being called to continue on the path to becoming a spiritual director? I offered a few examples. I talked about how I find myself using the principles of holy listening with my children and my husband. I described how I find myself talking less with friends and listening more, allowing them room to share and myself room to reflect before responding. I talked about how writing, my primary vocation, and my spiritual direction training inform and enrich each other. I also talked about what it means for me to commit, mentally and spiritually, and not just temporarily.

Ever since adolescence, my spiritual restlessness has compelled me to look for a path, a framework, a way of life that I could commit to. I tried the way of the artist, the intellectual, the hedonist, the rebel, the homemaker, the mother, the wife, the church community member. I know writers who say they would lose their identity completely if they couldn't write. I know intellectuals who frame the world in analytical terms, social activists who live for their causes and engage the world as gladiators in the political arena, women who unleash their creativity in their cooking and their houses. I know artists who immerse themselves in their personal creative angst to the exclusion of the rest of the culture, the rest of humanity's struggles. There are teachers who have made education a religion, social climbers who obsess about clothes and money and status, and ecologists who see the world in terms of a battle for the life of the planet.

I am beginning to experience my relationship with Christ as nonnegotiable. It's not always comfortable.

I have ended up being all of these things to some degree at one time or another, and none of these things to a complete degree, not to the very depths of my soul. Even as a wife, I can't and won't ask my husband, much as I love and honor and cherish him, to fill the empty place we all have in the depth of our being, because no one can do that for another. The only role I would lay down my life before giving up is that of mother, and even that identity will evolve and in many ways diminish as my children grow up. Everything else, up until now, has been negotiable: even writing, even Christianity, even Christ.

Ron Rolheiser, in his book *Holy Longing,* talks about the "non-negotiables" of Christian spirituality. I am beginning to understand what he means.

Becoming a spiritual director has slowly changed that "take-it-or-leave-it" sense of trying on various identities. I'd spent the first year of the training thinking about whether being a spiritual director was a practical choice for me as a career, as well as something I would find enjoyable, comfortable, and meaningful. Yet somewhere along the way I found that I moved from thinking about spiritual direction as a vocation, just one choice among many, into experiencing it as a way of life in all its human aspects, as well as a pathway to a more intimate relationship with God. I am beginning to experience my relationship with Christ as nonnegotiable. It's not always comfortable. I am asked to move into the very center of human experience in order to connect with God, and human experience often consists of suffering. It's not very practical. Certainly it's no way to make a full-time living. It's meaningful, but not necessarily in ways that are immediately apparent. Instead, moving into this new way of relationship with Christ and the world is a decided step into mystery. A step I am willing to take and more than that, from which I am unwilling to turn back.

On Choosing a Spiritual Direction Training Program

I first heard about the Mercy Center in Burlingame, California, and its spiritual direction training program over twelve years ago. At the time, cost, personal circumstances, and a muddled sense of who I was and in what direction I wanted to go kept me from exploring the program further, though I felt drawn to spiritual direction as a vocation. When I did finally apply for entrance into the program three years ago, I had done some homework. I read their program information, read a book on spiritual direction, researched programs on the Internet, and asked around for personal insights about spiritual direction in general and Mercy Center's program specifically. I am fortunate to live within a twenty-minute drive of a program that has been a good fit for me, and that the cost is within financial reach. Some aspects of choosing this particular program I hadn't even considered at the time I applied (but which are glaringly obvious to me now) include being in sympathy with their stated beliefs about prayer, contemplation, and social responsibility; the amount of time commitment involved; and, most importantly, their high standards of ethics and professionalism. We may be called by God to follow this path, but the human concerns of moral and ethical behavior, tolerance toward others, and defined and clearly stated expectations and learning objectives help shape an inner longing into a responsible and pragmatic outcome.

On the Street
Where I Find Myself

The more attentively I dwell in my place, the more I am convinced that behind the marvelous, bewildering variety of things there is one source.

—Scott Russell Sanders, *Writing from the Center*

The contrast between the Mercy Center, where I am training to be a spiritual director, and the street where I live, is stark. The Mercy Center sits on several acres in the city of Burlingame, one of the priciest and most elegant neighborhoods in the Bay Area. The buildings are surrounded by large, old trees and grassy lawns, and nearly every room in the center has a pleasing view. Set in the heart of an established upper-middle-class neighborhood on the mid-Peninsula, the grounds are quiet, graced with eucalyptus and live oak, and the sunlight fairly hums with contentment. The parking lot, set at a discrete distance from the main building, holds mostly newer sedans, the occasional minivan, sometimes a small truck or two.

I live about twenty minutes by freeway from the Mercy Center, in Daly City, one of the poorer cities in the Bay Area where houses are cheaper than in Burlingame, expensive only in comparison with the rest of the country. We live in a very small house with a large yard. Our street is narrow and crowded with cars parked bumper to bumper, so that people driving through have to slow down and edge by each other if they want to be careful;

then there are those who always drive too fast. Old, beat-up cars rest on blocks in driveways here and there, and the occasional Harley roars by, setting off car alarms. There are no trees to speak of. Abandoned shopping carts often pile up on the corner, and on weekend nights we sometimes close our windows against the shouting and boom boxes thumping through the neighborhood. The lawns range from raggedy with weeds to neatly trimmed, teenagers skateboard down the middle of the street shouting and swearing at each other, and in the summer we are more often than not blanketed in dreary fog from the ocean a mile away.

I have tried to practice embracing where I live as a worthy manifestation of God's gift of life and nature and community, and sometimes I rest in that sense of groundedness.

When I first started going to the Mercy Center I had to spend several minutes trying to release my envy and resentment of such a beautiful setting. Having lived in so many places, I am perhaps morbidly aware of houses, scenery, and neighborhoods. I've read many authors, such as Scott Russell Sanders and Annie Dillard, on discovering and claiming a "sense of place." These writers always seem to live in rural settings or close to them, where they reflect on the rivers and vast woods. I wonder how it would be for them to write a book about the wondrous nature to be found in the working-class neighborhoods of America. I have tried to practice embracing where I live as a worthy manifestation of God's gift of life and nature and community, and sometimes I rest in that sense of groundedness. Then again I often find myself railing at the overcrowded streets, the noise, and a lack of aesthetic beauty. Nature's glories are more subtly on offer on my street than in the country or the wilderness or at the Mercy Center. A cat sleeping on a warm sidewalk, flowers in a window box, the sky at dusk — these are the things of nature that inhabit my daily world, and I am often restless for more. Never mind hoping for immersion in wilderness; I'd settle for a tree here and there. It's like wanting to be in love and yet willing to settle for a friendly face. There are worse neighborhoods, of course, that reflect real despair. People here hold jobs, the houses mostly hold large, multigenerational families who seem to get along, and the graffiti is kept to a minimum. We know the people who live near us and exchange cards and cookies with them at Christmas. Our backyard has hosted many a game of tag and running through the sprinkler. I have learned to appreciate these things, and I am (mostly!) grateful for the lesson.

My ex-husband and I bought this house when I was pregnant with our second child. When we divorced five years later it became mine, and yet with no money and a foreclosure looming because of several missed payments, I nearly lost ownership altogether. My new husband, Andy, my knight in shining armor, poured his savings into the house, paid the back taxes, paid for a new roof, fixed a broken window here and a leaky faucet there, and here we are, several years later, still remaking the house into our image of a home together, bit by tiny bit. It was hard to stay in a house where I had been so unhappy, hard to not start over somewhere fresh. I had to remake my home from the debris of a failed marriage, like rebuilding at the site of an earthquake, or a war. I prayed a lot, and over the years the traumas and joys have merged into a life lived, instead of a life lost.

We still live in this house, in the neighborhood, for several reasons. Most of all, we are still here because the children can grow up in one place. Having moved so many times as a child, I am glad they have had the stability and familiarity of home. We could move to the edges of the Bay Area, to a larger house in a newer neighborhood (though new housing tracts don't have trees either), but we hate the idea of commuting. We are settled in the Bay Area, for now, with the kids happy in their schools, and their dad nearby so they can visit. And we are simply outpriced here; our house, which would buy a house double its size in the Midwest, is all we can afford, and given housing costs in the Bay Area, we are lucky to have it. I also sometimes wonder if we live here because I need to learn how to reach for Christ in the midst of resentment and restlessness. I've grown to be grateful to have a home when so many don't. I am grateful to feel safe in my family's love. I have learned how to take what I've been given and to create it anew. I am given the opportunity to look through Christ's eyes when I see the young mother of three pushing her children in a shopping cart to the apartments nearby, and the teenagers in those silly drooping pants who hang out at the nearby playground after school. We are all in this together.

I pray for gratitude, and I pray to not resent people who live in nicer houses, on quieter streets. I pray to not wait for an aesthetically pleasing setting to know God. I pray to center myself in this house, this neighborhood, this part of the world, this life. I ask Christ to meet me in my restlessness, to help me discover what it is I am actually restless for: a bigger house, a fancier neighborhood, a closer, more enveloping experience of nature? All of these would be nice, but none of them guarantee that I will meet God. Even the Mercy Center can't guarantee that. It's up to me to make the approach, from where I live.

Christian in the Creative Community

Why is it that I, who have spent my life writing, struggling to be a better artist, and struggling also to be a better Christian, should feel rebellious when I am called a Christian artist? Why should I be reluctant to think or write about Christian creativity?
— Madeleine L'Engle, *Walking on Water: Reflections on Faith and Art*

During my hiatus year from spiritual direction training, my spiritual and creative restlessness, which had previously found an outlet in the workshops, readings, and prayer, came unmoored and left me feeling edgy and impatient for change, for meaning, for direction. One day, searching the Internet for something that might catch my interest, I came across a website which included an opportunity to participate, via e-mail, as a trainee volunteer in an online training program for creativity coaches. Free coaching on creativity and writing — how could I resist that? During those three months I exchanged several dozen e-mails with Jori Walker, a woman training as a creativity coach living halfway across the world from me. I have never met or even seen a picture of her, yet I felt and still feel so indebted to this woman who took the time to read what I wrote about my struggles with the creative process, who humored me, cajoled me into writing beyond my comfort level, and generally took me seriously as a writer. I benefited so much from this e-mail relationship that I decided to train to be a creativity coach myself.

The three-month course consisted of weekly e-mail lessons, to which we were asked to respond in an online discussion forum, along with working with our own volunteers. I liked the material and its focus on the life of an artist as an ongoing decision to become what I think of as "a meaning-maker." By choosing to create, we choose to matter, to imprint ourselves on the world, to join the human conversation. I was so delighted and challenged by the training that I went on to take the three-month advanced training course. Making a living as a creativity coach, I have come since to realize, is about as practical as making a living as a spiritual director, but the teachings and the demonstrable effectiveness of partnering someone who is trying to create pulled me onward. After all, as a writer, I was used to embarking down paths that offered no viable, practical outcome in terms of financial support. I followed my interest and hoped for the best.

By choosing to create, we choose to matter,
to imprint ourselves on the world, to join
the human conversation.

Yet having just spent a year in a spiritual direction program where the focus was always on the spirit at the center of all human experience, I kept looking for the same thing in the creativity coaching lessons. I found myself saying more and more in my own postings to the training group about the intersection of creativity and spirituality. I argued for the inherent meaning in all work created through the spirit, and against the tendency to elevate "creativity" as a religion or process in and of itself, rather than a vehicle by which we connect with what I persistently called "the creative spirit." During that year I came up with the idea of starting my own website, one where I could begin to put my beliefs about creativity and spirituality into practice. I kept the terminology used throughout the site deliberately vague. I wanted my site to be for people who could accept the basic premise that the creative path and the spiritual path are most authentic, most immediate, and most transformative when they intersect.

When I returned to the spiritual direction program, I kept the site going. I felt that my training in creativity coaching enriched the direction training, and in fact the two aspects of approaching and engaging with God creatively and spiritually were (and are) for me inseparable. Meanwhile something was happening in my spiritual direction process that I could not continue to ignore as the owner of a website devoted to spiritual creatives. I began to accept Christ as the one who I want to behold. Now, on the Internet and as a writer and creativity coach, using the more general language of the present-day spirituality movement is one thing; naming my own faith practice as Christian or my own spiritual quest as that toward Christ is another. As a writer, I am sensitive (morbidly so, perhaps) to the way my message or any message is transmitted and received. I know that I can't control the outcome of what I write. The responses will be as individual as each reader. Yet unless a group is openly identified as Christian (as in the writing groups available online through Yahoo and other browsers for "Christian writers"), to move from talking about "the spirit" to talking about Christ is a big leap in the creative-spiritual community. It's a way of defining yourself that potentially leads to assumptions, pigeonholing, and the random, unintended opening and closing of mental, emotional, creative, and spiritual doors. It's as if I want to say, "I'm Christian. But wait! Here's what I mean by that."

In my course on spiritual writing, I counsel against using language that sets off alarm bells in the reader. I advise against preaching and using religious jargon. I speak to the practice of inclusion, remaining nonjudgmental, and being sensitive to how people might react to labels and language closely identified with any particular faith. I am going for the universal, rather than the particular as a way to reach more people, to exclude fewer. Yet in my commendable desire to be inclusive and welcoming to all of those on a spiritual and creative path, have I painted myself into a corner? Does this approach close my own door on the path I now choose, the light that beckons, the Christ?

In the last few months I have begun exploring how I might become a Christian in the larger creative community. I have an image of a line of people, and we are asked, "Everyone here who is Christian, stand over here." I move, then I look and see those in the original, larger group, and I miss them and want to be with them. I move back. Then away again, longing to follow my path. This group or that group is not better or worse, just separate — too separate. I want us all in a circle, gazing at each other on equal terms. I want to step into my identity as a Christian without losing connection with those who choose another path to God. I think that this can be done if I am willing to remain creative, flexible, and in good humor. How I will work to keep the connections open in my own work and my own aspect will simply require all my creative attention, and a lot of prayer.

The Practical Side of a Spiritual Life

Once women begin to answer the question "What do I most deeply want?" they then need to trust that this is also what God wants for them. Such trust rests on the conviction that being authentically myself and being the person God wants me to be are one and the same.

—Kathleen Fischer, *Women at the Well: Feminist Perspectives on Spiritual Direction*

Making the bed one morning I am suddenly struck by an insight, and a fresh perspective toward how I might approach Christ during prayer begins to glimmer. I keep making the bed, but my consciousness is focused far inward. Then my daughter appears in the doorway, upset about something a friend said to her. What can I say in response, "Not now, honey, I'm contemplating"? Clearly I'm not busy, just making the bed. Making an instantaneous choice, I return to the immediate present and respond to her dilemma. This is my spiritual practice of living in the real world; learning how to shift back and forth between pondering something in my own consciousness or in my heart, while simultaneously being present to my family and my responsibilities. Being a practical sort of person, I take a minute to write down a few words to remind me of what my insight was, and I leave the room to start dinner. Being on a spiritual path and becoming a spiritual director can't be adjacent to my life; they must become part of the weave of my life. Sometimes the dance between them is daunting.

In year two of the training, in between the more abstract topics of marginalization, prayer, and discernment, we also get to the basics of practicing being a director. We are required to work with a minimum of two directees until year three, when we are required to work with three to five people. Time becomes an issue. Two hours a month to actually meet with directees; time before and after each meeting to prepare and then to process the experience. I spend a couple of hours a month writing up the verbatim account which I will send to our supervisor, for discussion at a monthly meeting. The workshops we attend run from four to six hours a month, and then there's the books we read and the reflection papers we write. I figure that the actual time requirements directly related to the training, depending on how much time we spend on writing, reading, and reflecting on our experience, add up to about twenty hours a month. This doesn't include our own prayer time, outside reading or writing about our spiritual path, or general contemplation about spiritual direction as a calling and a practice. For those of us who work, who have families or community obligations, finding a way to integrate the training experience into daily life can be quite a challenge. Beyond the defined set of tasks we are given, and the hours spent directly related to training, we are challenged to incorporate our growing focus on this new way of responding to God into our everyday lives and relationships.

As we move into seeing directees, practical issues loom. How do you advertise for directees? Do you place an announcement in the church bulletin? Those among us who already work in ministry have a built-in pool of people we might work with, but other issues arise. Will there be a problem of a dual relationship? What about confidentiality? How do you switch roles? Those of us who are laypeople have to be more creative in how we might go about finding directees to work with. One person in our group feels that having to do the footwork of locating directees doesn't feel like a spirit-led process. Others ask friends for referrals or put an announcement in a church newsletter. I take the middle path, both practical and prayerful. I meet with my parish priest to share my intention of finding volunteers to work with, get his approval on the brief announcement I've written for the Sunday bulletin, make up some flyers for the back of the church, and then I turn the results over to God. "If you want me to direct people," I address God, "then send me someone to direct, and I'll do my best." Two people call me within a couple of weeks of the announcement appearing, so I'm all set. (And I breathe a sigh of relief that placing my trust in God worked out as I had hoped.)

For those of us who work, who have families or community obligations, finding a way to integrate the training experience into daily life can be quite a challenge.

Once I had two people to see, another practical concern immediately arose. How do you set up your meeting space? When spiritual direction was a ministry practiced solely by nuns, priests, and ministers, I imagine that the practical aspects of actually doing direction were less problematic. The nuns at the Mercy Center, for instance, have lovely offices to meet people in, while some of us in the training, myself included, make do with our living rooms. We have to spend time straightening up, cleaning the bathroom, turning off the phone, and shooing our families out the door. Preparing the space is part of the ritual and I don't mind it, but there are challenges nevertheless. During my first meeting with a directee, hoping for complete silence in which we could be reflective and prayerful, I turned off all phones, but forgot my cell phone, which rang in the middle of the hour. Another time, during a few moments of quiet, I heard my son's parakeet flying around loose in his bedroom, picking up and tossing a small ball with a bell inside. He managed to toss it several times against the closed bedroom door, right next to the living room. Fortunately, my directee was deeply absorbed in her story, and I was only distracted for a couple of minutes.

Parakeets, needy children, a tired husband home after a long day of work, cooking dinner, answering the phone — these are the spiritual companions and practices of my life. Yesterday, set to meet with a directee at ten in the morning, I dropped my children off at summer camp and should have made it home with forty minutes to spare, time enough to turn the chairs to a more intimate arrangement, adjust the blinds against the morning sun, and clean the bathroom. Just enough time to start making a cup of peppermint tea, and to begin thinking about the meeting ahead, and entering a more prayerful stance. Then the summer camp counselor called to say my daughter wasn't feeling well, so I went out the door, picked her up at camp and got back to the house with only a minute to spare, just enough time to put my daughter in my bed with some juice and the TV remote, close the door, and greet my directee at the door. No time to ease into a contemplative mind-set, no time to make or drink some tea, but time enough to be present with this woman who has come to see me, as we place ourselves before our God. Such is the spiritual practice of daily life.

Holy Listening
The Art of Spiritual Direction
by Margaret Guenther

There are as many good books about spirituality and about spiritual direction by women as by men, and one of the best is by Margaret Guenther, an Episcopalian priest, wife, mother, teacher, and spiritual director. *Holy Listening: The Art of Spiritual Direction* grounds the practice of spiritual direction in the realities of daily life, while allowing room for the mystery. Using examples taken from meetings with directees, scripture, and her own life, we are privileged to have access to Guenther's "Sophia" wisdom, or the feminine aspect of God. I felt encouraged by this book as a woman making my way as a fledgling director in a patriarchal religion. Yet when I wrote a reflection paper on this book for my training program, I took issue with her extensive use of midwifery as a metaphor for the work of a spiritual director. Even with having had two children of my own and appreciating a feminist perspective, I found the metaphor to be too narrow, too exclusive. Is there a feminine approach to spiritual direction? I am, at this point in my life anyway, too restless to want to wander for long down the narrow paths of gender consciousness, though God clearly has many faces, and Woman is one of them.

The Unpredictable Spirit

*Create in me a clean heart, O God, and put a new and right
spirit within me. Do not cast me away from your presence, and
do not take your holy spirit from me.* —Psalm 51:11

Teresa Blythe, a friend of mine who is a spiritual director and an
author, e-mailed me the other day. Having recently moved with
her husband to another state, a major transition in anyone's life,
she finds her inner state matching her outer situation as she tries
to make a new home and find a new paradigm for her writing
and her calling as a spiritual director. During seminary training,
she struggled with the question of whether or not to seek or-
dination. While for most people in seminary this is not even a
question, for my friend Teresa nothing is predetermined or in-
violate from the process of discernment. Now she finds herself
questioning her calling as a spiritual director. She wrote, "I don't
even know if I'm a spiritual director anymore—I have no clients.
I think I use a spiritual director's 'lens' to view the world, and that
is valuable."

She is also frustrated with her writing career right now, and
went on to talk about the different kinds of writing she might now
pursue. As her writing friend, I am interested in her analysis of the
various writing avenues open to her, and I could happily spend a
few hours debating the pros and cons of journalism versus essay
writing, or the secular markets (better pay, fewer religious ethics)

versus the "spirituality market" (little pay, more values). We could examine her writing career in terms of what excites her, what success she has had in the past, or where she might make the most money for her effort. We might be able to predict with some success how these various possibilities would pan out, given our combined knowledge of the marketplace. This is the tactic I would use as her writing mentor. Her situation is not unique or even uncommon. Most writers struggle with these issues from time to time. Am I in the right genre, how can I make some money to support myself, what am I interested in enough to write about? All creative effort includes an element of the unpredictable, which is what makes it interesting and alive. We learn to trust the un-predictable, and even to court it and invite it into the process. However, because of the tenuous nature of success, we do our best to predict and control marketplace outcomes ahead of time, in order to avoid heartbreak and wasted effort, and financial strain. Haven't I tried to find the same balanced combination of risk and control in all aspects of my life, from relationships to careers, to my life in Christ?

Teresa's restlessness reverberates in my own spirit, even from a thousand miles away. My intuitive response to her dilemma is that her restlessness is not generated by her questions about writing and spiritual direction, or at least not at its core. The con-cerns about money and success, though valid, are a symptom of a deeper restlessness, not the cause of her questioning. Instead, her spiritual restlessness is stirring up and challenging her previous notions about how her career would proceed.

This has always been true for me, and because of that inner knowledge I can see this same struggle in Teresa. It's about want-ing to be in alignment with the Holy Spirit, passionately desiring a connection from our own creative spirit to the Creator. Once we have made that connection the path from here to there becomes clear, because the creative restlessness that compels us to keep seeking more will naturally and spontaneously find a medium through which we can express the fruits of that generative connection. It's not a once-and-for-all decision, but a process we continually revisit throughout our lives, as the spirit-led wilderness we travel through offers us both closed and open doors.

All creative effort includes an element of
the unpredictable, which is what makes
it interesting and alive. We learn to trust
the unpredictable, and even to court it and
invite it into the process.

Connecting with the Holy Spirit, the source of creativity, isn't a one-time event, isn't static but fluid, as we continue to be creative, not just created. I have complete faith in this process, because I know from experience that it works. I can't *think* my way into right alignment with myself and my Creator. I can only place myself in the heart of the desire. For Teresa as well, I believe that it's a matter of placing herself in her deepest desire in the presence of God, and being completely open to the unpredictable outcome. She could bring to God the Creator her fears and concerns about writing, about her calling as a spiritual director, her general unease and restlessness, and listen for what resonates in her heart.

After reading Teresa's e-mail, I took a few minutes to imagine myself sitting across from her as her spiritual director. What would I say to Teresa? Fortunately for me, this is an exercise in futility. I can't think my way into an answer for her, because the answer is not mine to give. However, I might offer her the opportunity to take some time, as we sat together, to move more fully into that desire. Asking Christ to guide us, we would move from there to an outcome I can't predict here, because God's movement is unpredictable, creative, and occurs beyond the limits of thought, place, and time.

On Writing This Book

When the editor of this book, Roy Carlisle, contacted me after reading an essay I'd written for the e-mail newsletter that *Sojourners* magazine publishes ("sojomail"), I was delighted. He wanted to know if I had thought of writing a book. I had thought of it actually, and in fact, had been thinking about it for over two years. I wanted to describe and share this vague idea I had about how restlessness might not be something to avoid or "cure," but rather an indicator of God's presence and thus a condition to be embraced as a spiritual path toward commitment. I initially showed him a proposal I'd put together on the compensations of restlessness, but the overall approach felt too commercial to both of us — too much like a self-help book, a format which required that I know all the answers. As we talked, it became clear to us that the greater challenge and yet more interesting book would center on my stumbling steps toward spiritual commitment. I am a learner, not a preacher or professor, and so I embarked from the perspective of student rather than expert, much to my relief. Writing the book amidst the daily tasks of parenting, teaching, marriage, and all my other roles served to keep me grounded in the ordinariness of a spiritual life. After all, I hadn't met Christ while on a silent or cloistered retreat, so why should writing a book about meeting Christ be any different? One myth about the writing life is that it must be secluded, sanctified, absolute in its intensity and focus. I have found this to be true *while I'm actually writing*, but not while living a writer's life.

I wanted to describe and share this vague idea I had about how restlessness might not be something to avoid or "cure," but rather an indicator of God's presence and thus a condition to be embraced as a spiritual path toward commitment.

As I wrote this collection of reflections, there were times when I hesitated. I asked myself, "Do I really want to reveal my struggles, my doubts, or my dubious status in the Catholic Church? Do I really want to reveal what a novice I am at spiritual direction, or what a long way I still have to go? Do I really want to share my story?" Yet every time I thought about holding back, avoiding a topic, or watering down the truth of my experience, my restless eagerness to explore the new territory of God motivated me to keep going. I realized that if I profess to believe that the most important task in becoming a mature adult is staying true to oneself, to discover and live an authentic life in alignment with the Trinity, then I have to walk the talk. The process of writing this book became a container, a compass, and an ever-renewed source of vital energy for my spirit, and for that I am eternally grateful.

In the Night

Forgetting all, my quest
Ended, I stayed lost to myself at last.
All ceased: my face was pressed
Upon my Love, at rest,
With all my cares among the lilies cast.
— St. John of the Cross

My intention in these reflections is not to be relentlessly positive about spiritual restlessness. On the contrary; spiritual restlessness can be frustratingly uncomfortable, which is why I suspect many people try to tamp it down. That discomfort is after all what motivated me to seek out a way to transform a state of being fraught with tension and ambiguity into something useful. I just didn't realize when I began that the usefulness I sought would lead to Christ. I imagined, in my limited way, that I would perhaps find a place in the world to finally put my overflowing reserves of energy to good use, to create something successful out of my restlessness and thus of my life. And I have done that, here and there. I've become a spiritual director intern. I've made connections with people and ventured into relationships with friends and strangers. I started a successful website, did volunteer work at my church and my children's school, and pushed my own comfort level to tolerate a wider embrace. But these are the results of a more essential encounter with the One who stirred me to restlessness in the first place, not the endpoints in and of themselves.

I feel the restlessness most urgently in my body. When I lie down at night I feel relaxed at first, ready to sink into the comfort of cool sheets and soft pillows. Yet more nights than not, it only takes a few minutes before my nerves begin to vibrate with a subtle yet relentless movement, and my muscles begin to want to move. Then I am up and out of bed, roaming into the living room, stepping out onto the front porch to look at the sky, picking up and putting down books, and peering into the quiet rooms at my sleeping children. Am I restless because I need to get more exercise during the day? This might be part of it, but not all of it. Am I restless because of work undone, regrets remembered, anxiety about the future? This could part of it too, but not all of it.

My intention in these reflections is not to be relentlessly positive about spiritual restlessness. On the contrary; spiritual restlessness can be frustratingly uncomfortable, which is why I suspect many people try to tamp it down.

What can one do in the middle of the night? I can't meet with my spiritual director or wake my dreaming husband for a chat. I can't attend Mass or volunteer my time with children or look into the eyes of a stranger. These things by day offer a way to channel my restlessness into close human contact and contact with God, but at night, it's just me here in this house, and I am less sure of how to move from my self-contained, inescapable restlessness to communion with Christ. I can't settle down long enough to write, because my mind is active but not focused enough, and I have nothing to say anyway. So as a last resort, I try prayer. During these agitated times I remember other times of greater crises, when money was scarce and I felt great physical fear. The only thing that worked then was sending up a prayer, born of desperation and barely articulated. "Please, God. I am at the edge. Help me survive this."

Now though, I try prayer without words. Sitting still, or kneeling, I simply allow myself to sink into the restlessness that pervades my heart, my body, my spirit. I become still in the center of the restlessness, open to it, aware of it, but not consumed by it, because I am simultaneously offering it up to God, asking Christ to be present with me in my restlessness. "Here I am Lord," becomes my only articulated thought. Not, "take this away," or "help me survive it," just offering my longing, my desire, my restlessness in its entirety, without expectation. I turn toward my restlessness instead of trying to fix it or escape from it.

Sometimes I just go back to bed, finally tired enough to sleep, though I may sleep fitfully. Other times, I can feel something begin to seep into my nerves and my muscles, a sensation like entering a warm, scented bath. Not a release of tension so much as a renewal of spirit. The restlessness becomes less like anxiety and more like hope. Less like stress and more like creative energy. Less like loneliness and more like companionship. I become less a stranger to myself, more true to myself, and yet less self-absorbed, more aware of the world all around me. My restlessness has brought me to my knees, and to Christ.

On Prayer

Prayer is to spiritual direction as physical exercise is to health. We practice prayer to build strength for the spiritual journey, to keep the channels of our spirit open to God's grace, and to stay connected with who we are in God's sight. As a trainee I've learned about various beliefs, practices, styles, and outcomes of prayer, both from differing traditions and personal perspectives. Because the Mercy Center program is centered in the Christian tradition of spiritual direction, we often discuss and practice traditionally Christian forms of prayer, from Lectio Divina to centering prayer. I've been impressed by how the program leaders manage to share their beliefs about prayer, without "telling" us what to believe, how to practice, or what to expect as a result. In this way they are modeling the work of spiritual direction: they create opportunities for approaching the Holy, offer some suggestions for ways to go, but the decisions are between us and our God. Lately I've been having these glimpses in my imagination of a prie-dieu, which is a kneeler for prayer. Does this mean I want to build one and put it in the corner of my living room? What would my kids think of that! I do think it means that I'm attracted to a more committed stance before God in my prayer, one that moves beyond praying while doing the dishes or in other, more casual circumstances, into a physically embodied acknowledgment of my attentiveness to Christ.

Why This Church, This Pew, This Faith?

At that time Jesus went through the grainfields on the sabbath;
His disciples were hungry,
and began to pluck the heads of grain and to eat.
When the Pharisees saw it, they said to him,
"Look, your disciples are doing what is not lawful to do on the
*   sabbath."*
He said to them, "Have you not read what David did
when he and his companions were hungry?
He entered the house of God and ate the bread of the Presence,
which it was not lawful for him or his companions
to eat, but only for the priests.
Or have you not read in the law that on the sabbath
the priests in the temple break the sabbath
and yet are guiltless?
I tell you, something greater than the temple is here.
But if you had known what this means, 'I desire mercy, not
*   sacrifice,'*
you would not have condemned the guiltless.
For the Son of Man is lord of the sabbath." —Matthew 12:1–8

A friend of mine and I were chatting outside of the school gym the other night, killing time while our younger daughters practiced volleyball and our older kids practiced teenage socializing, whatever that is! It can be hard to tell, given the jokes and slang and teasing flying around from girls to boys and back again. As my friend and I talked, the subject of high school inevitably came up. We each have a teenager starting their frosh year in the fall at a Catholic prep school, an honor they worked hard for and which we will pay dearly for, given the tuition costs. The fact that our kids are Catholic was a factor in their acceptance, of course. As I pointed out to my friend, "over 80 percent of the kids who are attending there are Catholic." And then I made a comment that, even as I said it, stunned me in its cynicism. "After all, we should get some benefit out of belonging to the Catholic Church, given what else we have to put up with."

My friend just laughed, and the subject moved on to something else, but my comment continued to echo in my mind long after the evening was over and I had driven the kids back home. For me as a spiritual director, the particular faith tradition I belong to is not essential to what I do, but the commitment I have made to that faith is. Because spiritual direction is not just about theology but about how we encounter God, I don't have to examine my theology (much) when I am directing someone. Their theological understanding might come into play if it impacts their ability to enter into the presence of a loving God, but I am not there to set them straight on some finer doctrinal point, or to make sure they are practicing their faith accurately. I do have to have an understanding of what I believe about who God is and how God moves in our world and in our being, but this is more personal than theological understanding, based on experience seasoned with reasoned understanding as opposed to learned doctrine. Still, for me as a spiritual director and as someone seeking God's presence myself, what container I choose for my own committed faith journey is a relevant (if somewhat daunting) ongoing subject for my own discernment. Obviously there is some examining on my part to be done, otherwise that caustic comment which my friend just laughed off wouldn't have caught me so off-guard and wouldn't still bother me.

Why am I in the Catholic Church? Or a more accurate question to ask myself might be, "Why do I attend a Catholic church?" This is a question I can only answer for today, not for the rest of my faith life, since that path is still evolving. So for now I certainly belong to a Catholic parish where I attend Mass, serve as a Eucharistic minister, and light candles as part of my prayer practice. Yet I don't think of myself as irrevocably Catholic, beyond the immediacy of my parish involvement. Irrevocably Christian? Yes. If asked, I tell people that I am Christian, currently committed to a Catholic parish and community. So if after thirteen years of attending Mass I don't think of myself as Catholic with a capital C, why have I committed myself and my children to attending Catholic Mass, and why do I send my kids to Catholic schools, where they receive the sacraments and volunteer as altar servers? What would it take to be irrevocably Catholic? Perhaps it would take a closer joining of who I am and who the Roman Catholic Church says I am.

I converted to the Catholic faith during my previous marriage (my ex-husband was an Irish Catholic), seeking something more concrete than the "higher power" of Twelve Step programs. I was restless, looking for a faith challenge, wanting more from church and a faith tradition than I had known as a Protestant. Restless for a container of tradition and ritual to hold my desire for God, I became Catholic one Easter vigil night, thirty-one years old and eight-and-a-half months pregnant with my second child. Much of that experience is now a blur, tired as I was from chasing a two-year-old child around and trying to cope with running a business, an overworked husband, and an uncomfortable pregnancy. Later, I kept attending because I wanted to raise my children in a faith tradition, and I liked attending Mass. When I chose a school for my kids, I wanted a Catholic school so that they could hear the words of faith in a daily context. The statue of Mary in the foyer of the school, the messages of God's love as a natural part of the classroom décor and school message made me feel welcomed. I took the kids regularly to the 10:00 a.m. "family" Mass, bringing coloring books and stuffed animals to occupy them during the homily. I began to make friends with other parents, to recognize faces, to know people I could smile and wave to who would smile and wave back.

For me as a spiritual director, the particular faith tradition I belong to is not essential to what I do, but the commitment I have made to that faith is. Because spiritual direction is not just about theology but about how we encounter God, I don't have to examine my theology (much) when I am directing someone.

Now, thirteen years, one divorce, and a new marriage later, I still attend Mass, still occasionally say the rosary with the seniors in our congregation before 9:00 a.m. weekday Mass, and still receive Communion. Here is one major roadblock where the Roman Catholic Church and I part ways: to the church, because I divorced and remarried without the absolution of an annulment from the church, who I am is someone who is not supposed to receive Communion, not welcome at the Eucharist. Yet in the restlessness of my heart where Christ resides, who I am is someone worthy of

God's gift of the Holy Supper. In my own heart, I am a member of my parish and of the Catholic faith and as such I am worthy to receive Communion. I can be at peace with this because I am not thinking about what the church says about who I am, not always easy for someone who thinks so much and relies on the gift of reason as a significant pathway to God. I respond to the call to Eucharist because Christ loves me as I am, and because my restless spirit won't let me sit passively and submissively in the pews. Of course, some in my faith community, including the priests, might have real trouble with this, and although my status has been private up until now, something between me and God, this essay will change that to some extent.

Part of becoming a spiritual director, however, has included an ever-growing confirmation that Christ asks only that I be my most authentic self. To pretend in these pages to a status in the church that I am not granted would be hypocritical, and feels too much like cooperating in a kind of "don't ask, don't tell" scenario. I know other women who receive Communion yet feel unworthy because of their marital status; others have just stopped attending Mass altogether. I imagine this is not an uncommon situation for countless people, and I find that unbearably sad. What would I do if I were directly told by my parish priest that I am not allowed by the dictates of the church to receive communion? Would I sit quietly in my pew while others go up to receive Christ's blood, Christ's body? Would I try to get an annulment, something that feels intrusive and emotionally destructive of the fragile peace my ex-husband and I have worked hard to obtain? Neither of these options feels right to me, in my heart, in my spirit.

I have to admit, sometimes I wish I were more sanctioned by the church as a worthy member. Then things would be straightforward. If I were to seek an annulment, which I would most likely be granted given the circumstances of my marriage, I would be following the rules. It would be great to belong, to feel part of the included instead of one of the defiant, but my restless spirit tells me that obeying the rules is not always the most direct path to Christ.

For me as a spiritual director and as someone seeking God's presence myself, what container I choose for my own committed faith journey is a relevant (if somewhat daunting) ongoing subject for my own discernment.

As I continue to I think about why I belong to a Catholic faith community, arguments spring to mind both for and against continuing to do so. Reasons for include the fact that the Catholic Church has fostered great thinkers, activists, poets, contemplatives, and saints who move and inspire me. The church's tradition of working for social justice is unrivaled, except perhaps by the Quakers. Being a member of the Catholic Church has forced me to confront my own self-centeredness, my own fear and antagonism toward people who are different from me, and has taught me to see myself as one person committed and connected to a larger community, with its attendant responsibilities and rewards. On a personal level, I like the people in my community, and the pastor is a wise and compassionate presence. Reasons against: nearly every social doctrine, including church attitudes toward celibacy, women, homosexuality, procreation, and barring remarried people from celebrating the Sacrament of Communion.

In the end, I don't attend my local church because of something the church hierarchy has done or not done. What religious institution doesn't have flaws, secrets, isn't dysfunctional to some extent? In fact, if I were to think too much about what denomination to give my loyalty to, I would end up belonging nowhere, because no denomination totally meshes with my own belief system. This is not to say that I advocate joining a church blindly, without serious reflection, intellectual consideration, and sound judgment. Nor do I think that "cafeteria Christianity" is a final solution, since at the core of the Christian faith is a courageous willingness to stop roaming and start joining. A reluctance toward commitment has never brought me into sustainable contact with Christ. At parish community events and during worship, I meet Christ. In my neighbor next to me in the pew, in the pastor of the church, in the music and the communal celebration of the Eucharist, Christ is present.

Where I choose to belong has to do with how I choose to love. While I continue to study other faith traditions, both Christian and non-Christian, and while I might at some future point look around at other faiths and visit other churches if I decide I need a better fit intellectually, socially, politically, or even musically or aesthetically, for now those considerations would serve only as distractions from this central truth; what I most desire is to learn how to be in Christ. For now, all other considerations are, at this time in my life anyway, on hold. So why am I committed to the Catholic Church or more accurately, to my parish church? Because that is where I can give and receive faith, hope, and love. A commitment to my faith community has rewarded me, as a spiritual director, with a strong sense that I am connected through that communal relationship to God, which in turn helps me to connect with my directees in the light of God's loving presence.

The Church, Abuse, and Choice

For me as an adult convert to Catholicism, allegiance to the church is not "bred in the bone." The church has not shaped my essential religious identity from childhood. The sex and power abuse scandal that has permeated the Catholic Church and devastated everyone from lay members of congregations to the highest clerical authorities has not deeply impacted my feelings about being Catholic, nor has it made me want to leave the church. At least, not yet.

I have not felt compelled to leave, for several reasons. First, because I am not surprised by the revelations of abuse and cover-up. Saddened and angry, yes, but not shocked or disillusioned. Priests, bishops, and all those in holy orders or clerical power have never been sacrosanct to me, just human and thus imperfect and subject to sin. Second, I don't imagine that there is any another denomination that is free from its own history of abuse — perhaps not to the same extent, but all institutions are susceptible to the corruption of power. Third, this is not an issue that hits close to home, as self-centered as that may sound. My parish has remained relatively untouched, and I don't know anyone personally who has been directly affected. I more seriously considered leaving when I read that the Vatican was considering banning girls from altar-serving (they have since abandoned that move), because I can't imagine asking my daughter to participate in a church that wouldn't consider her worthy enough to serve at Mass. I am deeply distressed and angered by the subservient role assigned to women, more than I often care to admit to myself. Yet, I stay for now because I love my parish and I don't feel compelled to leave — that is the long and short of it.

I can understand why someone would leave the church, if the abuse to their sense of self, their body, their spirit, or even their intellect became so damaging that God was no longer reachable in a Catholic context. So the question and the answers, for me, of why I am a member of the Catholic faith are still evolving. I feel as though I walk a tenuously thin line of commitment to my church, balanced between heart and mind, between sorrow and joy. What dysfunction and sickness will I tolerate, if not for myself, than for my fellow Christians, for the sake of the greater good the Catholic Church offers me personally, as well as the larger Christian community? I don't want to turn a blind eye, or collude in not demanding change. God has given me the ability to choose and the means by which to make decisions if I pay attention to the signals from my heart, mind, body, and spirit. For now, I want to belong to this faith tradition. So I continue to notice and reflect on the ever-evolving nature of my faith, my place in the Catholic Church, and my relationship with Christ. I am so grateful that I am not required to meet God only in the structures and grooves of an imperfect and flawed religious institution, since Christ surpasses all attempts to define, capture, and legalize his presence, his word, his love.

Accepting the Open Door
of Who I Am

Jesus keeps saying this: that he has come to search out what is lost, to find and heal the broken-hearted, to bring good news to the poor. That is what Jesus is here for — unconditional love. God just keeps devising more and more mysterious and humble and spirit-filled ways to get us to be human and love back.

—Megan McKenna, *Parables: The Arrows of God*

A large part of our direction training focuses on who we are as individuals, not just on what the skills are that we need to learn as directors. We are counseled to first understand ourselves in order to better understand who we are in relation to our directees and in relation to God. The clearer I can be about who I am, the clearer I can be in my reflections and responses to my own self first and then to others. So who am I in and of myself, before I enter into roles with others, as mother, wife, friend, daughter, colleague, spiritual director?

Among other things, I am a thinker. I am on several daily e-mail lists devoted to Christianity, from a Christian writers' group to "Christianity Today." Because I love books and discussions about the Christian faith, I could spend hours each day reading about church history, following ongoing doctrinal discussions, enjoying church gossip, and pondering social-political issues related to the church. And sometimes, I do just that. I read and think and read some more. I can follow nearly any argument, comprehend obtuse points of doctrine, and empathize with personal narrative.

Yet, while I am a thinker, I am not an intellectual. Not being of a scholarly bent, I tend to absorb huge amounts of information and then promptly forget many of the salient details, like names and dates. I can't recall who said what to whom. Having spent much of my adult life lamenting my inability to recount facts on demand or demonstrate total recall of texts, I've now come to believe that this intellectual "weakness" of mine has saved me from the seduction of the intellectual life.

The clearer I can be about who I am, the clearer I can be in my reflections and responses to my own self first and then to others. So who am I in and of myself, before I enter into roles with others, as mother, wife, friend, daughter, colleague, spiritual director?

Not that the mind is not a path to God, but it is ultimately not my path—only a detour. I've learned to accept the fact that certain doors are forever closed to me: the doorway into academia, into intellectual acclaim, into scholarship. It has forced me to accept that while I might like to think and read and write about God and faith, my path to God is not the intellectual path. I am forced back toward my own self, which is smart but not dazzling, intelligent but not scholarly, communicative but not brilliantly persuasive.

Another aspect of who I am is a sensual mystic, whom I define as one who communes directly with God through the senses and

body-awareness. I am willing to know God through direct communion of my body, mind, and heart, as opposed to indirectly through
literature and philosophy. My senses won't be ignored, as I meet
God in water and earth and the touch of another. My heart won't be
quieted as I meet God in my children and husband and in all human
suffering and joy. While the life of the senses is another kind of seduction, capable of being misleading in its intensity, distracting in
its passion, and I am easily seduced by romance, this is a path I
can learn to walk with eyes wide open toward a more encompass-
ing union with God, through the immediacy of human contact and
interaction. Yet because I am at this point in my life sensual but
not ecstatic; more detached than engaged in the textures, sights,
tastes, and sounds of God's creation, I am thus limited in my ability
to surrender to a certain kind of transcendent experience.

I thought for many years that I might want to be a minister, a
pastor. However, while I like ministering to people, I get nervous
when I have to speak in front of people. Until recently, even getting up to serve as a Eucharistic minister made my heart pound
with anxiety until I learned to ask Christ to be with me in my nervousness. I've had to accept that while I like to talk with and am
comfortable with all kinds of people, I am basically shy when it
comes to having to take the stage. I've come to accept that my
role is on the sidelines of community, not out in front. Where does
this leave me in relation to the calling of spiritual direction? As
we are reminded in our training, spiritual directors are not called
to preach. We are not called to minister. We are not called to provide intellectual responses to questions about doctrine. We are not
called to engage another in human contact, sensory union, or to
enter into states of transcendent ecstasy. We are simply called to
listen and to love. We bring whatever gifts we have to bear; for me
that includes all of my life experience, my own relationship with

God, my reason and common sense, and my sense of humor. As much as I might want to dazzle with my knowledge, reap the accolades of clever discourse, achieve transcendence, experience God through sensuality, or shepherd a pastoral community, I am only asked to meet one person here and now, to be fully myself, and to be open to God in every aspect of my being. All considerations of intellect and personality aside, this is challenge enough for a lifetime. So my weaknesses become my strengths, as I move around the seductive detour of intellect which in my case is a blind alley, across the minefield of sensuality, through the thickets of wanting to be capable of more than I am, into the more rigorous path of "who I am," called to place my imperfections and limits in the service of Christ.

On Finding a Director

Finding a director who is a good match and helping a directee determine if I am a good match for him or her is a delicate dance, one I'm still learning. Like any relationship, if we are too much alike, we don't encourage each other to grow beyond our own comfort levels into deeper communion with each other and with God. If we are too different, we can't find any common ground on which to establish basic trust. This holds true with pastoral leaders as well. I find it easier to have a spiritual experience during Mass if the priest's approach toward God and toward faith does not diverge too much from mine. Fortunately, the process is not just orchestrated by two imperfect individuals — God has a hand in it as well. I've learned much about what kind of director I want to be from my own directors. For instance, as someone who likes to talk, I'd always thought I'd want a director who likes to talk too. Lately though, I've realized I need to learn to trust the silence. A director who will sit in contemplative silence with me gently "directs" me toward a more fulfilling path by doing so, when I might have filled that silence with words.

———

Fortunately, the process is not just orchestrated by two imperfect individuals — God has a hand in it as well.

———

That said, it would be easy to shop for directors the way we sometimes shop for the perfect church, or the perfect pastoral leader — not staying long enough to gain the spiritual sustenance that commitment brings. Praying about it, talking honestly with a director, asking ourselves how we feel, helps with the discernment.

Practicing Prayer with a Moose and a Frog

Knowing she would be
My counselor in prosperity,
My comfort in cares and sorrows
— Wisdom 8:9

My daughter Claire mentioned in passing one day that she had written a poem, but that she wouldn't show it to me because she didn't think it was any good. I didn't press her on it, or offer that automatic mother-response of "Oh honey, I'm sure it's wonderful," and the moment passed. Later that night, preparing for bed and worried about a long trip she would be leaving for in the morning, she began to fret. She was already homesick, she said, and a ten-day trip without me seemed like too much. Knowing she was near tears, I tried to not just blandly reassure her, or distract her, or dismiss her fears casually. Then, in the midst of the emotional storm, she mentioned her poem again. Knowing that something mentioned more than once is something worth paying attention to (which I learned from my spiritual direction training), I asked her what the poem was about. It was silly, she assured me. "I'd like to read it, if you'll let me," I offered.

Her focus shifted from her anxiety about the trip to her own creativity, as she got out her notebook and scanned the poem. I waited a few minutes while she crossed out and added a line or word here and there, absorbed in her work. Then she handed me

117

the poem and as I read it, I realized why she had felt uncomfortable with it. "This feels very different from what you have written before. The rhyming is more subtle, and the lines flow in a different way. It feels like maybe it's a song. Maybe these are lyrics more than just a poem. What do you think?"

I knew when I saw the recognition dawning in her face that she agreed, and that she had known something was different, but not why. Her discomfort at venturing out into a more challenging and more evolved way of writing was a result of not knowing what it meant or where it had led her. Now, when she thought of her work as lyrics, it all fell into place. She said that she didn't have any music for it, and doubted she could ever write any, so I suggested that she just enjoy the new process that was beginning in her writing, without worrying too much about where it might lead her and whether she was up to the challenge. Meanwhile, as we focused on her poem, her emotions shifted and the anxiety that had overwhelmed her became manageable. We sat together companionably with our stuffed animals, me holding a tiny purple moose and Claire holding a large green frog. We talked about writing, and how poems sometimes come naturally, and other times we have to work harder to make a connection with our creativity or our "muse," but that practice makes that connection stronger and easier to call on when we need it.

As I made motions to leave her room and go to bed, she started to get upset again. "Why don't we pray about it?" I suggested. "That helps me when I feel like there is something I just can't handle. We can pray together, right now." I took her hands and said a quiet prayer out loud, something about asking God to "Be with Claire as she struggles with her fears." Then I looked at her and smiled, but she wasn't buying it.

"It doesn't work, Mom, I've tried that before, and I don't feel any better." She didn't seem upset, just exasperated. "Well," I joked, "you mean I'm writing a whole book about being with God and you're telling me it doesn't work? I'd better call my editor and cancel the contract!" She laughed, and so did I. "Listen honey, maybe it's like taking an Advil when your braces hurt your teeth. It doesn't work instantly, but a while later you realize that you feel better." She looked skeptical. I tried again. "Or it's like what we said about writing poetry. Sometimes we are given a poem without even thinking, it just happens as something we call 'grace.' But mostly we have to practice, to keep writing or in this case, praying, and as we go we develop a stronger connection with God that we can call on when we need it."

That gave us both something to think about as I settled her in with the moose and the frog, and I kissed her goodnight. When I checked on her a few minutes later she was already asleep. I, however, stayed awake long into the night, but that's another story.

Singing in the Spirit

Make a joyful noise to the Lord, all the earth.
Worship the Lord with gladness;
come into his presence with singing.

—Psalm 100

I once heard a hospital chaplain explaining why he often sang to the people he visited. As I understood it, he believed that sometimes people needed comfort but not advice, solace but not speech. My experience of rocking my babies to sleep years ago bears this out — when I sang "Swing Low, Sweet Chariot," I could feel them relaxing into my arms. Making up songs worked best when they were older and an earache or cold kept them awake; listening for what might come next out of Mom's mouth distracted them from the irritation and pain. But when they needed soothing, nothing worked better than a familiar tune with its gentle promise of love. Pain became tempered by melody. Preschool had the best songs to offer: the banana slug song, the "Hokey Pokey," and the ever-popular "This Little Light of Mine," the best part being, of course, the obligatory shout on "Put it under a bushel? NO! I'm gonna let it shine!"

Our spiritual direction workshops often start or end with the group standing or sitting in a circle and quietly singing a few verses of a simple chant. When I'm feeling rebellious, I imagine breaking out into a rousing gospel tune, clapping hands and shouting a few "Hallelujahs!" but I don't do this, of course. We do have lovely church voices, and once in a while someone ventures a harmony while we sing, "Sacred is the call, awesome indeed the entrustment; tending the holy, tending the holy." Our music and musical style is what you would expect from a contemplative group and it's pretty, but sometimes I wish we would break out of character and give a joyful shout, or add a drum beat. Music works best when the spirit breaks through spontaneously, with an unexpected harmony, a graceful gesture, a taste of passion, an unexpected emotional emphasis.

One Christian line of thought says that singing is as much a part of the worship experience as prayer is. Well, of course it is! Just look at a gospel choir, moving and swaying their bodies into the very soul of a song, united as one joyful body in Christ.

I've thought a lot about that chaplain, singing to the people he visits who are sick or dying. I wonder what he sings. I imagine they request a song sometimes, or he offers one. He'd mentioned that sometimes the family members gathered around the bed would join in; other times it's just him singing by himself, although I don't think he's alone in spirit when offering up his voice. I've wondered what it would be like to sing with a directee. We are encouraged to open and close our sessions with a few moments of silence, followed perhaps by a prayer either offered by the directee or by the director. What if the two of us were to sing a verse of a favorite hymn? I am so often moved in church by the hymns we sing, and when I am thinking of a prayer I might share, often a line from a song is what first comes to mind though I don't suggest it, at least I haven't until now. "And I will raise you up," or "You are the center of my life," or "Here I am Lord." We might not get up and dance about, we might not to all outside appearances be having rousing fun, but I can imagine the joy we would feel.

Music works best when the spirit breaks through spontaneously, with an unexpected harmony, a graceful gesture, a taste of passion, an unexpected emotional emphasis.

There is something very intimate about singing, and I often feel so grateful when I look around in church and realize that a room full of people are all singing the same tune, not communicating with each other directly, yet united in this harmony, these words, this rhythm. Not everyone sings, of course. One Christian line of thought says that singing is as much a part of the worship experience as prayer is. Well, of course it is! Just look at a gospel choir, moving and swaying their bodies into the very soul of a song, united as one joyful body in Christ. Sometimes the passion is less evident, driven into the depths of the sound by a certain disciplined restraint, yet we are no less focused on what we are offering up. When the choir I traveled to Europe with sang a Gregorian chant, written for the very cathedral in which we performed, the echo caused by the acoustics would send back to us the line we had just sung, now layered on top of the next line. This echo could have as much as a seven-second delay, carefully accounted for by the composer, so that a harmony we sang built in four lines would suddenly sound in eight lines, and we became more in that moment than we actually were, as the past seven seconds merged with the present seven seconds into one glorious, extended, celestial tone.

Not all music is blessed, not all music is a vessel of God's light or a joyful shout. The intention toward transcendence isn't always there, either in the construction of the tune or the performer's heart. Some music generates a dark undertow of passion and seduction which, if heard by a lonely and uncentered soul, does nothing to heal and brings no joy. As an adolescent, I found that music became a solace in my loneliness, and while some music comforted me, more often it stirred desires that were ungrounded in the Spirit. Rock and roll is not the devil, but anything that so deeply penetrates the senses without being centered in God is ultimately empty. Oh, but the lyrics, the deep bass guitar, the drum beats pounding and reverberating in your very bones! There must be a compromise somewhere between Nirvana's "Smells Like Teen Spirit" and "Tending the Holy," between Gregorian chant and hip-hop. Music is a gift from God, a pathway to God, and it's yet an imperfect human medium, vulnerable to tedium on the one extreme, and unanchored, irresponsible, and meaningless passion on the other. Yet, as the hymn says, "how can I keep from singing?"

Practicing Prayer, Take Two

Once I was complaining to a wise friend that I often awakened at about two o'clock in the morning and then could not get back to sleep. The friend asked me if I really wanted to know why I awoke. I did want to know, for the days after these sleepless nights were a grim ordeal. So he told me that God wanted to talk with me.

—Morton Kelsey, *Set Your Hearts on the Greatest Gift:
Living the Art of Christian Love*

In talking and being with my daughter the night before her trip, I practiced many aspects of being a mother, as well as those of a spiritual director. We laughed together; she focused on where she best engages with the Spirit (in her creativity); and I spent time listening and meeting her where she was, instead of trying to force her into an emotional state that might have been more comfortable for me but would have been only a temporary fix for her. The hardest part of motherhood is accepting the fact that I can't take away my children's suffering. If I could, I would lift it from them as if it were a burden wrapped around their shoulders and place it on mine instead. I've come to realize over the course of these last fifteen years of motherhood that there are many things my children must confront on their own without me, but it is harder to trust that they are not alone, but with God. They are traveling with God just as I am. Yet hard as it is to trust the truth of this companionship in my own life, it is even more difficult to trust that it is true for my children.

My own childhood memories hold an aura of loneliness. Despite various relationships with men and friendships with women as I got older, I didn't feel connected to anyone or anything in a real sense until my late twenties when I found my way to Al-Anon. Even with the wisdom of the Twelve Steps and the program to guide me, I still mostly felt that it was up to me, and only me, to steer the course of my life and by extension, my children's lives. When I managed to surrender my need to try and control people, places, and things, real transformations would occur. Yet with each new situation I would grab control again, or at least the illusion of control. Where does personal responsibility, for myself and for my children, end, and trust in God begin? Figuring out the balance between my part and God's part in the dance of life is a lifetime task. As I practice being a spiritual director, I realize that this task faces me each moment with my directees as well. Where does my part begin and end? I don't want to neglect my part and thus allow any unnecessary suffering or feeling of loneliness when I could do something to alleviate it. But how do I know when suffering has a place in someone's life that is beyond my comprehension, a spiritual condition that is part of the Mystery?

Figuring out the balance between my part and God's part in the dance of life is a lifetime task.

On this particular night, as my daughter slept, I expected to fall into bed and sleep immediately. I had been rushing around all day, getting her and my son ready for the trip. Remembering each little item from bathing suits to toothpaste, folding the clean laundry and hunting up batteries for their CD players, reassuring them that they would have a good time. When they fell asleep that night I read for a few minutes, kissed my husband goodnight, and sighed into my pillow. An hour or more later, still awake, I eased myself gently out of bed so I wouldn't wake him up, and resigned myself to a night tossing and turning on the couch. As the night progressed I felt more awake, not less, as my mind conjured up images of what might go wrong on their trip. Outlandish, irrational fears that no doubt every parent has experienced, from worrying they might get sunburned to envisioning a car accident and being notified by the police of their death. I ventured deep into over-the-top, out-of-control worrying. It felt like a fever washing over me, as my mind raced. I ventured further out in my worrying to more distant themes of poverty and war and illness. I was plunged into my worst personal struggle with God — my inability to trust that if I let go of feeling constantly vigilant, everything will be all right. Because after all, my own experience tells me that it isn't true; things aren't always well and good and all right. People trust God and still experience suffering.

Yet I also know from experience that my physical presence, my prayers, and my vigilance are also no guarantee that everything will be "all right." I can't follow my children around, can't cure the world of disease and violence, can't protect anyone in the larger sense, just as my physical presence and prayers with my directees can't guarantee that their suffering will end.

I had a brief revelation that night which I struggled to hold on to: that being a mother who doesn't drive herself crazy with anxiety means assuming the mantle of a new level of trust, a challenge I will no doubt visit and revisit, again and again. Trusting that God is in charge and that I am only required to show up, to be there when needed, and to let go when it's not my turn, not my task, not my place.

Mostly I can do this in my life. I let go, I don't try to "push the river," and I practice surrendering my will. But this night, events and emotions and who knows what else conspired to send me into the familiar and blind corridors of helplessness and fear. So I tossed and turned and looked out the window and paced up and down, and thought about this tempestuous relationship I have with God. I felt Christ, there, patient and solid, and me, truculent and off balance. God wasn't absent that night; God was a punching bag for my fears, a patient listener as I rambled on, a friend sitting up with me through the night. I was Jacob wrestling in the dark, and sore in the aftermath: heartsore.

My husband said to me the next morning, as we stood in the kitchen and I told him how I had wrestled with my demons, or was it God, in the night, "we can't fully be with anyone in their suffering and take it from them, even if we hold them in our arms. And that's all right. They really aren't alone, we aren't alone."

I looked at him.

"You don't get what I'm saying," he said quietly.

"Oh, I get it," I replied. "I'm just not there yet."

Later of course, the storm of my anxiety subsided. It eased because I had leaned back against the hand of God, not just because I was worn out, or the clock ticked on, or I forgot about it. I was thankful for the steadfastness of Christ's presence, the patience of my husband, the love of my children, and the chance to try once again to trust.

Discernment

Jesus bent down and wrote with his finger on the ground. When they kept on questioning him, he straightened up and said to them, let anyone among you who is without sin be the first to throw a stone at her. And once again he bent down and wrote on the ground.
—John 8:6

Christian spiritual direction relies on certain essential practices that guide both the director and the directee on the spiritual direction journey. One of these key practices is a process called "discernment." This is spirituality language for making a decision that is grounded in a sense of God's will for us. When I think about the decisions I've made in my life, it's sometimes hard to tell which ones were made in conscious alignment with God's will. I have found myself in situations that must have been the result of a decision at some level of consciousness, but more often it's felt like a line from "Once in a Lifetime," a Talking Heads song: "Well, how did I get here?"

In John 8:6, we see Jesus drawing in the dirt. What is he doing and why? I've come to believe that Jesus was taking his time, slowing down the hasty actions of others, and discerning how he might respond to their harsh judgment. As I've learned how to be a spiritual director and as I have grown in my own spiritual life, discernment has come to mean, for me, examining on *all* levels what I might do next. Not just on a thinking level, not just on a visceral or intuitive level, but bringing my whole self to the process of knowing where I most need to go, how to get there, and inviting God into the experience. Some decisions have been more about practicalities than desires, or more about emotional needs than common sense, and I am now the sum of all these actions and inactions. Learning how to discern in the presence of God, before deciding what to do in the world, has helped alleviate the sense of life as a roulette wheel.

I've made some decisions in my life after carefully *thinking* through all of my options. Getting a master's degree in education is a good example. I examined all of my academic options, looked at the practical aspects of the time commitment (I could attend classes at night, and because I worked at a university, my boss agreed to let me take three hours a week during the work day for class) and money (tuition was free because I worked full-time at the university), and I studied the course catalog to see if I could cobble together a program that interested me. I had wanted very much to go to seminary, but as a single working mom with two young kids I couldn't afford it, and this seemed like the next best thing. After all, we might "discern" what we want to do, but the world may have other plans. I'm glad of the results of the path I took, but my options were not wide open at the time so I made the best of things. Discernment doesn't necessarily mean freedom of all choices, just the freedom to make the best choice of the options available with God's help.

I've made other decisions based on a gut reaction to someone or something. I've been forced to a cliff edge of panic and desperation and jumped, hoping for the best. I've put off decisions until they made themselves, for better or worse. I've made so many major decisions at this point in my life — where to live, what work to do, what friends to have, what church to belong to, whether to marry, to divorce, to marry again, to have children, to become a writer, to become a spiritual director, and so on, not including the multitude of small decisions that we all make every day—that to even begin to question them now would take up the rest of my days. Some of these decisions felt God-infused. Many of them did not, at least at the time. I wasn't even aware that turning to God was an option, so how could I have been aware that God was present? Yet whether or not I was conscious of it, God was there in each moment, in each turn of the road. What I hope for now is to become ever more aware of God's presence as I live each moment and reach each time of choosing, so that I can discern the choice that is most in alignment with the path toward Christ.

As I've learned how to be a spiritual director and as I have grown in my own spiritual life, discernment has come to mean, for me, examining on *all* levels what I might do next.

In Nora Gallagher's most recent book *Practicing Resurrection: A Memoir of Discernment,* she grapples with unraveling the various components of her desire to enter the Episcopal priesthood. Her journey is a long and thoughtful one, both painful and joyful. When I first heard about her book, before I had even read it, my first reaction was, "Why of course; if you could choose seminary and ministry, why wouldn't you? How lucky she is to even have that choice before her!" This response, of course, says more about me than it does about Nora or her book. It tells me that some part of me still longs for the path of religious study and ministry. It must, however, remain an open-ended, long-term subject for discernment for me, because these things do not loom on the near or distant horizon. I allow this sense of distant possibility to live in my heart, because as I grow in God's presence I find room for all options, and the patience and trust I need to let things unfold.

When I meet with my directees I am aware of this elastic aspect of discernment. Some things loom large and immediate for them: should I stay with my partner, should I change jobs, what can I do about my health? Other issues have a more leisurely yet no less meaningful aspect to them: how might I begin to do some creative work; how might my prayer life begin to assume a more central place in my life; how will I approach this next stage in my aging process? Recognizing the breath of God in each movement of our lives, the sense of pressure and urgency lessens, and life seems less like a board game with a race to the finish line and more like a painting, as we work with the colors, the medium, and the canvas before us that is our life. Time opens up, as we become active participants with God, in how it unfolds, how we decide, and how we respond.

Hearing with the Heart
A Gentle Guide to Discerning God's Will for Your Life
by Debra Farrington

Spiritual direction, both in training and in practice, centers on the spiritual process of discernment. *Hearing with the Heart* suggests many different ways of looking at how discernment might operate in our lives. While discernment requires a certain trust in the Mystery, it also has its practical components that this book addresses, including how we can calm our minds and begin to order our thoughts and feelings in such a way as to better hear God's voice. Her teaching on skills versus gifts is the most insightful I have ever read on how we can discern the difference between what we are capable of and what we most desire.

Because for much of my life I operated by moving from crisis to crisis, coming up with short-term solutions that led to unhappy, long-term consequences, I have only recently come to terms with the aspect of spiritual discernment Debra describes that insists on allowing enough time for things to unfold and be revealed. Leisurely time for contemplation or discernment had been a luxury during those times when I lived hand-to-mouth or in physical or emotional crisis. Discerning which job to accept is moot when you are desperate for any work that will pay for food and shelter. I've taken jobs I hated because the rent was due; moved to a new city because a friend was going that way and I needed to leave home; made decisions about relationships in a few weeks that should have taken several months or years. God was there in each decision, but I didn't bring my full, attentive, contemplative self to the process. Yet if discernment could become a natural a part of our spiritual practice at even a young age, how might such a life unfold? I wish I had Debra's book at hand many years ago, but perhaps I wouldn't have been ready for it then. I am learning at a steady pace now, learning to lean into the rhythm of God's time, which is neither too fast, nor too slow.

Taking It on Faith

Now faith is the assurance of things hoped for, the conviction of things not seen. —Hebrews 11:1

Here's the part of believing in God and the living presence of Christ that I most take on faith. As I wrote earlier in this book on the topic of discernment: "I wasn't even aware that turning to God was an option, so how could I have been aware that God was present? Yet whether or not I was conscious of it, God was there in each moment, in each turn of the road."

I know this and I wrote it so confidently, and yet I don't *always* know it. I can remember so many moments in my past of trying to see which way to go, of feeling like it was all so hard, of feeling anxious and fraught. I also remember clear moments of joy, of the rightness of a course of action or the peace of a task well done, a friendship made, a poem written. Was God there in all of it, the good and the bad? How do I know? Because my spiritual director thinks so? Is it like the song, "Jesus loves me, this I know, because the Bible tells me so"?

When I entered the spiritual direction program, I wanted perhaps above all else to know God, and more than that: I wanted to figure out where God had been all my life. Some people enter training already having a clear sense of God's presence in their lives. They have a well-developed set of spiritual muscles, so to speak, a working relationship with Christ. Perhaps this is a better, more advanced place to operate from as a director. Nevertheless, I entered in a state of restlessness, stirred from the center of my pelvis to my very fingertips by my desire to enter into a more authentic and holy alliance with God, but also unsure, resentful, eager, a whole hodgepodge of tangled love and desire. I knew God, but it was as a newly met, midlife romance, not as a lifelong partner. Like a jealous lover or an abandoned child, I wanted to know where God had been before now.

When I entered the spiritual direction program, I wanted perhaps above all else to know God, and more than that: I wanted to figure out where God had been all my life.

Being asked to examine the times in our past when God felt close was painful for me. The wise people of the program assured me that God *was* there, despite what to me seemed like all appearances to the contrary. The books I read on Christian spirituality said that God is always with us and so did my fellow-trainees when they shared their stories. I had to take it on faith. The inarticulate response in my heart felt so immense that I resisted it.

It was like being told that your parents, who left when you were very small, had been, unbeknownst to you, nearby all the time, and not only nearby, but actively loving you. The sorrow I have felt for the lonely child I was, has been hard to bear. I've been worried in retrospect for the safety of the adolescent I was, then young woman, then new mother. I found it hard to forgive myself for not recognizing God, to forgive others for not helping me to know God, and to forgive God for not trying harder to get my attention.

Yet being resentful and hurt had only taken me so far, and still God patiently waited, so I practiced letting go of what I know and what I don't know, and trusted that someone else might show me a better way to go.

Was God there in all of it, the good and the bad? How do I know?

What has ultimately worked for me in my desire to see God's mark upon my life has been a refocusing of the narrower lens used to examine discrete, unique experiences to a wider view that encompasses the broader landscape of my life. I can now recognize God in the themes that have permeated and shaped who I now am. I have discovered that my life is composed of restlessness; of a determination to take risks; of my great desire for more than what appears on the surface of things; of my willingness to love. I find a repeating chorus of creativity, playfulness, compassion, and love of the wilderness. If these things are part of me, and they are part of what I have come to know of God, then I am part of God, and God has always been here, intertwined in the fabric of my life, woven into the complex tapestry of who I am. Like a child who loves unconditionally, like a betrayed lover who risks her heart in order to love again, I take it on faith.

The Communion of Spirits

*For where two or three are gathered in my name, I am there
among them.* —Matthew 18:20

In our spiritual direction training, we practice spiritual direction
in an arrangement we call "triads." We are divided into groups of
three, with each taking the role of spiritual director, directee, or observer. We are then given a general focus for our practicum, such
as "praying in spiritual direction" or "discernment." Then we spend
fifteen minutes or so in a role-play. We don't choose which role we
will have in each triad; rather, we are assigned in careful rotation,
which pushes us past our comfort levels. Given the choice, I would
usually choose the part of directee, because then it's like getting
an extra session of spiritual direction. Some people much prefer
the role of director, because they don't necessarily want to get into
their own personal experiences right then and there. The role of
observer might seem the easiest, but I find it very challenging because we are expected at the end to describe what we observed
in a way that is insightful and helpful, so I really have to stay alert
and in a thinking mode, not always easy at the end of a long day.

Some of my most powerful experiences as a director have oc-
curred while in a triad with a fellow trainee. Because the people
who have sat across from me in triads have been as focused on
the spiritual direction process as I have for the last two years
of training, they are able to move to a place of concentration

and awareness in just moments, switching from workshop mode to contemplative silence and then into the heart of their experience. This transition always catches my breath, as we move from being genial colleagues having an interesting and enjoyable time together into people open to the presence of God. We enter into a current of the spirit and are moving along, not passively or helplessly like a raft bobbing on the surface, but like surfers who have caught a wave and attune their physical skills with the ocean's powerful motion. It reminds me of other moments when I have felt a shift in the current of God's presence, like the time my son sank two perfect free throws in a seventh-grade basketball championship game, in a moment of physical embodiment of spiritual grace.

To spend fifteen or twenty minutes with another person in alignment with God's presence is life-altering. In those sessions I have been given the gift of another person's honesty, vulnerability, and trust, and offered my own prayerful attention and love in return. We have both been blessed with an experience that is greater than the sum of our two selves. While as directee or director I am not focused on the observer, I believe that the observer's attentive and prayerful presence adds to the experience in incalculable ways as well. I would not want to learn how to do this work alone by reading books or sitting in a classroom. By practicing in triads, I both hone my skills as a director and stay in touch with what it's like to be the directee. As an observer I learn to recognize the skills involved in direction and to state those observations in constructive ways.

These opportunities are of immeasurable value, because although the emphasis in our program is on spiritual direction as a "calling," every calling must be shaped by the disciplines of learning, observation, and practice. As imperfect beings, we may feel called to serve something greater than ourselves, but that doesn't automatically mean that we are already perfected in our service simply by answering the call. In spiritual direction, as in writing, I have discovered a vocation that allows me to offer the best of who I am in a wonderful combination of my skills and talents and all-too-human imperfections, so that I can experience a lifetime journey of growth, exploration, and transformation. And just as I would not expect to write well without practice, revision, suggestions from others, false starts, overcoming doubts, and weathering the rejections, I don't expect to practice spiritual direction without lots of input from others, prayer, practice, humility, forgiveness, and study.

> To spend fifteen or twenty minutes with another person in alignment with God's presence is life-altering. In those sessions I have been given the gift of another person's honesty, vulnerability, and trust, and offered my own prayerful attention and love in return.

I'll never achieve perfection as a writer or a spiritual director, but after all, these are just vehicles for grace, not grace in themselves. These are ways and means toward the experience of God, conduits for my restless spiritual longing, not final destinations in and of themselves. So I practice, and take it seriously as well as lightly, and within the community of my fellow seekers, I find my way.

On Loving

And if I have prophetic powers, and understand all mysteries and all knowledge, but do not have love, I am nothing.

—1 Corinthians 13:2

When I sit in my chair across from someone who has agreed to meet with me for an hour to focus on her spiritual journey, I feel honored. I also sometimes feel nervous. Honored, because to speak of God is a precious and courageous act. Nervous, because I want to do my best, to be the best director for this person that I can be. If I remember to take a few deep breaths and to ask my holy companion, Christ, to be with me during this hour, in this moment, with this man or woman, then the nervousness subsides. I'm not in charge after all; I am just a gentle moderator, a tour guide along the way. I feel more confident, more relaxed, filled with love for this person and this process. I love the people who come to see me. I can't help it — they're lovable. Because I value opening my heart to encompass others not only during direction but as a daily spiritual practice, sometimes I can even extend that love to a person that I don't find lovable — someone I meet as I go about my day, or someone that I am tied to in one way or another. If I am willing, my own feeble attempt at loving is amplified and strengthened through Christ's love, which is the very definition of being a Christian.

Sometimes I have to settle for not actively judging or resenting people in my life or in my daily encounters, which is a far cry from loving them but the best I can do in a given moment. It helps if I practice detachment, which for me means not thinking that I have to control who they are or how they act, or what decisions they make with their lives. Then I am free to see them as people in relationship with God, not just inextricably bound up with me and what I want. Al-Anon taught me the most about this kind of detached, nonjudgmental loving. I loved someone and intertwined my identity with his so completely that I lost all track of time, purpose, and direction. Love was a candle burning in the wilderness, lighting the dark, calming our anxiety, keeping the demons of loneliness at bay. Yet love not contained within the holy countenance of God is an empty embrace.

One of the most important lessons I have learned about loving in the adult years of my life is that loving myself must rank right up there with loving someone else. That loving someone doesn't mean abandoning who I am and what I deserve as a child of God.

Through the loving, reasoned, practical guidance of a program that suggests detached love instead of control and offers acceptance and surrender instead of manipulation and willfulness, I learned to stop trying to make others conform to my image of them, whether they were on the "right" path or not. In doing so I was free to resume my own relationship with God, instead of putting all my energy toward trying to fix someone else's life. I had to let people stand and fall on their own merits, their own decisions, their own actions, as a sign of respect for them as adults and as people of God in their own right. I learned to set limits on my efforts to change others, and boundaries on their efforts to control and change me. I have enough to do staying on my own path, and if I can do that with any success, then by my example of how I live, not by my instruction, will I offer any wisdom that might come my way.

If I remember to take a few deep breaths
and to ask my holy companion, Christ,
to be with me during this hour, in this
moment, with this man or woman, then
the nervousness subsides. I'm not in charge
after all; I am just a gentle moderator, a
tour guide along the way.

One of the most important lessons I have learned about loving in the adult years of my life is that loving myself must rank right up there with loving someone else. That loving someone doesn't mean abandoning who I am and what I deserve as a child of God. Even my love for my children, which is as unconditional, fierce, and nonnegotiable a love as I have ever known, must at times be tempered with loving myself so that I set limits when I need to in terms of time and attention, and practice viewing myself as a separate individual with her own path. Loving them also means that while I may know what's best for them some of the time, that's certainly not true all of the time, and they have a right to their own identities, their own developing relationships with God. I'm still learning about love and hope to keep exploring its mysteries throughout the rest of my life. I have so much in my life now, through the gift of my marriage, my children, my friends and family, and through Christ, as I learn a little more each day what love requires of me. But for now, as a director, when I am facing someone who is sitting just a couple of feet away from me, a candle lit between us, the room quiet, love wells up in me, and I am visited by joy. I don't have to reach for it, and I don't attempt to block it. Why block a love centered in God? It's not as if there is enough of it in anyone's life. Loving as a human manifestation of God's love is the hardest thing to do consistently and well, much harder than judging or disliking. I need all the practice I can get.

Answering the Call

Now the Lord came and stood there, calling as before, "Samuel! Samuel!" And Samuel said, "Speak, for your servant is listening."

— 1 Samuel 3:10

Before I meet with a new person who is coming to me for spiritual direction, I spend time in prayer, asking God to help me bring all of my best self to the encounter, and to help us discern if we are a good match for each other. Then I let go of all expectations and greet her or him as a new friend.

As we meet over time and I get to know this person through our monthly conversations, I begin to recognize the pattern of my directee's life. I hold her in my thoughts and prayers when we are not together, so that I feel connected to her even after a month away. Although the topics may shift dramatically from month to month and the issues that seemed so pressing a month ago may have resolved or lessened, there is continuity in her journey. She may not see it. When we look at our own lives, they often appear fragmented, disjointed, speeding up too fast here, slowing down too much there. We leap from idea to idea, from plan to plan, trying this door and then that door. As this woman's spiritual director, I am listening for the persistent, underlying themes that create a unified pattern of meaning, because these are the moments, the feelings, the experiences that connect us to the spirit that pulses through all of life.

143

Sometimes though, we just laugh. I delight in my directee's stories. I'm happy for her, and I wish her well. Other times, more is asked of me, and it is in these moments that I find myself most challenged to stay with the process. These are the moments I bring to my supervisor to revisit and discuss. When we meet, we always read aloud a verbatim account I have written about an experience from one of my sessions with a directee that I want to explore during supervision. As we read, I am right back in the moment, and the feelings well up. And then the learning begins, as I begin to understand just what it is I am being asked to do as someone's spiritual director. I am there to listen, to enjoy someone, to pay attention to her feelings. I am there to model God's loving presence. I am there for all these things, because these are all the qualities of friendship. Yet while spiritual direction is friendship, it's much more than that. It's a form of holy companionship, but more than that as well. Let me offer an example of what I mean.

In each of our lives, we have experienced schisms in our relationship with ourselves and consequently with God. We have been subjected to or been the cause of events deeply painful to us, as fresh as when it began. We may or may not be aware of how we are still carrying that pain in our hearts. A divorce; a feeling we wish we didn't have, such as relief at someone's death; suffering abuse at the hands of another; abandonment; and so much more; the whole panoply of human suffering is accessible in each one of us, in one form or another. These moments are brought to me as a spiritual director and I know when they arrive, because the very quality of the atmosphere changes. This is true regardless of whether or not the directee is aware of it. I feel a physical shift in my awareness, as if God has prodded me to sit up and take notice, as if some vibration in tone that hums all around us has deepened in pitch.

I am not responding this way simply because someone has mentioned something painful. People mention painful things all the time. All you have to do is listen to your friends and family, and you will hear pain at some point in what they share. What I am responding to is the sudden awareness of an open, vibrating channel to God. In my deepest anxiety and restlessness I am closest to God and can connect with God if I am willing to move deeper into my suffering, and in so doing, move on through it and into the loving Presence. So too, such moments of relived and still vivid human experience are times when my directees can move into the presence of God. They may not recognize it. By bringing up the subject of something so painful that it blocks them from their fullest selves and from God, they are taking a risk, and this particular doorway to God swings shut quickly if we are not awake enough to recognize it and courageous enough to walk through it.

I am there to listen, to enjoy someone, to pay attention to her feelings. I am there to model God's loving presence. I am there for all these things, because these are all the qualities of friendship. Yet while spiritual direction is friendship, it's much more than that. It's a form of holy companionship, but more than that as well.

I have been offered these moments by my directees, and sometimes I have taken their hands, metaphorically speaking, and we have moved deeper into their experiences. I have gently suggested

145

we stay with the feelings. I have offered my own empathetic silence and prayer. I have been a silent presence as they have gone into themselves to live that painful experience fully, this time with an awareness of wanting to meet God. Other times, I have not been able to go the distance. Vibrating with the awareness of a significant moment, I have been sympathetic, but when a directee moves away from the pain, I go gladly with them. I disregard the truth which my own experience, my own sense of God, my own body, is telling me: that here, now, is a way into God. My whole being says, "This is important. Pay attention. Don't move away." And yet I do, or my directee does, and I follow her back into safer, less charged territory. Why do I hesitate, if only on the most unconscious level? Am I afraid of something? Of her pain, of what I am being asked to do? But I am not being asked to heal this person, to fix this person, to take away her pain. I could understand my quailing before that daunting task. Instead, I am being invited into the presence of God, and being given the opportunity to share this invitation with my directee as well, if she is so willing. Sometimes we may move away because God's timing is not right for this movement toward the center of an experience. The art of spiritual direction is about knowing the difference between our movement and God's movement and bringing them into harmony. I only hope that I will continue to be given such moments of grace. It's what I've been looking for in all my restless searching, if I can only respond to the call.

Our time together after these moments have passed is still meaningful, still helpful, still interesting and companionable. But God is fiercer than companionship, more awesome than interesting, more profound than our wisest understanding can imagine. Yes, I can offer my company; that is a particular gift of mine and I give it freely. God, however, is not mine to give, but sometimes

I am offered the grace to recognize God's presence, if only I have the willingness to trust.

> What I am responding to is the sudden awareness of an open, vibrating channel to God. In my deepest anxiety and restlessness I am closest to God and can connect with God if I am willing to move deeper into my suffering, and in so doing, move on through it and into the loving Presence. So too, such moments of relived and still vivid human experience are times when my directees can move into the presence of God.

As a spiritual director intern, I get to keep practicing how to not turn away from God. I also get to practice this as a writer, a mother, a lover and wife, a friend, and a Christian. Even after I complete the training program, I will seek out more experienced directors, both as a directee myself in relationship with a spiritual director, and as someone seeking guidance as I continue to direct others. I am grateful for the chance to meet with my supervisor to talk about how I might best serve my directees and nurture my own spiritual life. I am grateful that my directees come to talk about God in their lives, because as they find grace, I find grace. I pray and hope for more courage, more wisdom, more patience, and for the opportunity to meet God, so that I might take this restless self into the wilderness at the center of my heart and there greet and embrace my Teacher, my Healer, my spiritual director who is Christ.

Acknowledgments

Thank you, dear family, for putting up with the demands of a creative project. I also wish to thank Roy M. Carlisle, senior editor of Crossroad Carlisle Books, for contacting me out of the blue to ask if I wanted to write this book. His confidence in me and interest in what I had to say were inspiring. Allan Bruce Zee agreed to let us grace the cover of this book with his stunning photograph, for which we are all delighted and grateful.

I want to acknowledge the people of the Mercy Center for welcoming me into their spiritual direction program, their spirit-led community, and their hearts. To my fellow trainees, the spiritual directors, writers, teachers, pastoral leaders, and creative mentors who share their faith, enthusiasm, and gifts with me and in their ministries and in their daily lives, my deepest respect and gratitude. Especially Teresa Blythe, friend, fellow writer, and spiritual director, and Kay Porterfield, friend, author, and writing mentor extraordinaire. Thank you to my dear friend Mary Farrelly, who loved me and cared for me and my children through thick and thin. A special blessing for the many members of my parish community, especially Tina and my friend Eileen, who supported me and my family through good times and bad, and for all those who continue to offer their friendship, good humor, and commitment to all of us gathered as fellow members in the body of Christ.

About the Author

Sarah Stockton, M.A., is a spiritual director in training at the Spiritual Director's Institute at Mercy Center in Burlingame, California, where she will complete her three-year training in May 2004. She lives in the Bay Area with her family. She is also the founder and director of centeredpath.com, a website devoted to cultivating the intersection between creativity and spirituality and offering courses in writing and spirituality. She also teaches for the University of San Francisco.

Selected Readings

On Christian Spirituality

The Holy Longing: The Search for a Christian Spirituality, by Ronald Rolheiser. New York: Doubleday, 1999.

Letting God Come Close: An Approach to the Ignatian Spiritual Exercises, by William A. Barry. Chicago: Loyola Press, 2001.

One Like Jesus: Conversations on the Single Life, by Debra K. Farrington and Alan Jones. Chicago: Loyola Press, 1999.

Parables: The Arrows of God, by Megan McKenna. Maryknoll, N.Y.: Orbis Books, 1994.

Set Your Heart on the Greatest Gift: Living the Art of Christian Love, by Morton Kelsey. Hyde Park, N.Y.: New City Press, 1996.

On Spiritual Direction

Holy Listening: The Art of Spiritual Direction, by Margaret Guenther. Boston: Cowley Publications, 1992.

Inviting the Mystic, Supporting the Prophet, by Katherine Marie Dyckman and L. Patrick Carroll. New York: Paulist Press, 1981.

Women at the Well, by Kathleen Fischer. New York: Paulist Press, 1988.

On Discernment

Hearing with the Heart: A Gentle Guide to Discerning God's Will for Your Life, by Debra K. Farrington. San Francisco: Jossey-Bass, 2002.

Practicing Resurrection: A Memoir of Work, Doubt, Discernment, and Moments of Grace, by Nora Gallagher. New York: Knopf, 2003.

On Writing, Creativity, and Christian Spirituality

Imagination and Spirit: A Contemporary Quaker Reader, edited by J. Brent Bill. Richmond, Ind.: Friends United Press, 2003.

Mystery and Manners: Occasional Prose, by Flannery O'Connor. New York: Noonday Press, 1969.

Walking on Water: Reflections on Faith and Art, by Madeleine L'Engle. New York: North Point Press, 1995.

Writing from the Center, by Scott Russell Sanders. Bloomington: Indiana University Press, 1997.

For information on spiritual direction training programs or a referral to a spiritual director, contact:

Spiritual Directors International
PO Box 25469
Seattle, WA USA 98125
(425)455-1565
www.sdiworld.org

"Spiritual Directors International [SDI] is an ecumenical association of colleagues, grounded in the Christian faith, whose sole purpose is to serve the growing network of spiritual directors world-wide and the people who train them. The inspiration for this network began in 1989 at Mercy Center in Burlingame, California, USA." —*From the SDI website*

Mercy Center
2300 Adeline Drive
Burlingame, CA 94010
(965)340-7474
www.mercy-center.org

OF RELATED INTEREST

THE HEART OF HENRI NOUWEN
His Words of Blessing
Edited by Rebecca Laird and Michael J. Cristensen

Henri Nouwen is considered one of the greatest spiritual writers of our day, and is without question one of
the best selling, with titles such as *Life of the Beloved*
and *In the Name of Jesus* to his name. He taught at Harvard, Yale, and Notre Dame. To commemorate the 70th
anniversary of Nouwen's birth, Crossroad has issued
this remarkable anthology of the best of Nouwen's writings. Key themes in these writings include a personal
relationship with God, suffering, and living for others.

0-8245-1985-X, $19.95 hardcover

Paula D'Arcy
SEEKING WITH ALL MY HEART
Encountering God's Presence Today

A verse in Jeremiah promises that the seemingly elusive
God will be found when "you search for me with all your
heart." This collection of reflections and meditations is
such a search — a search that has taken D'Arcy through
both New and Old Testament, honored writings, as well
as the reaches of her own experience. D'Arcy shows
contemporary spiritual seekers that when we meditate
on these verses, our sense of time disappears and there
is only now. They speak, if we are willing to know and
to see differently.

0-8245-2109-9, $19.95 hardcover

crossroad

OF RELATED INTEREST

Richard Rohr
SIMPLICITY
The Art of Living

"Rohr's kind of contemplation is an adventure in the wilderness, letting God call me by name and take me to a deeper place of the peace that the world cannot give and can no longer take from one once it is encountered."
— *St. Anthony Messenger*

0-8245-1251-0, $17.95, paperback

Ronald Rolheiser
AGAINST AN INFINITE HORIZON
The Finger of God in Our Everyday Lives

Full of personal anecdotes, healing wisdom, and a fresh reflection on Scripture, *Against an Infinite Horizon* draws on the great traditions of parable and storytelling. In this prequel to the bestseller *The Holy Longing,* Rolheiser's new fans will be delighted with further insights into the benefits of community, social justice, sexuality, mortality, and rediscovering the deep beauty and poetry of Christian spirituality.

"Rolheiser has mastered the old, old art of parable."
— Morris West

"A felicitous blend of scriptural reflection, shrewd psychological observations, and generous portions of letters sent to Rolheiser and his responses."
— *Commonweal*

0-8245-1965-5, $16.95 paperback

crossroad

OF RELATED INTEREST

Ronald Rolheiser
THE SHATTERED LANTERN
Rediscovering a Felt Presence of God

The way back to a lively faith "is not a question of finding the right answers, but of living a certain way. The existence of God, like the air we breathe, need not be proven...." Rolheiser shines new light on the contemplative path of Western Christianity and offers a dynamic way forward.

"Whenever I see Ron Rolheiser's name on a book, I know that it will be an amazing combination of true orthodoxy and revolutionary insight — and written in a clear and readable style. He knows the spiritual terrain like few others, and you will be profoundly illuminated by this lantern. Read and be astonished."
—Richard Rohr, O.F.M.

0-8245-1884-5, $14.95 paperback

Rita Winters
THE GREEN DESERT
A Silent Retreat

The Green Desert is the story of one burnt-out ad exec's silent retreat in the Sonoran desert. This heartfelt diary of fifteen days in the desert chronicles Rita Winters' inner journey out of a comfortable life to start over again in midlife. "It is only when you retreat that you can truly go forward" (Rita Winters).

0-8245-2133-1, $18.95 paperback

crossroad

OF RELATED INTEREST

Thomas à Kempis
Consolations for My Soul
Meditations for the Earthly Pilgrimage
toward the Heavenly Jerusalem

Translated by William Griffin

Next to the Bible, *The Imitation of Christ* is the bestselling
book of all time. What most people don't know is that
the book's author, Thomas à Kempis, wrote other bril-
liant works, including *Consolations for My Soul,* which
has been unavailable to readers in our day. In this new
translation, Bill Griffin has captured the charm and deep
spirituality of this monk, with wisdom about God and
the soul's mystical relationship to the divine.

0-8245-2107-2, $19.95 paperback

Please support your local bookstore,
or call 1-800-707-0670 for Customer Service.

For a free catalog, write us at

THE CROSSROAD PUBLISHING COMPANY
16 Penn Plaza, 481 Eighth Avenue
New York, NY 10001

Visit our website at
www.crossroadpublishing.com
All prices subject to change.

crossroad